VATICAN

St. Peter's Basilica
The Vatican Museums
The Sistine Chapel
Inside the Vatican City

Lozzi Roma
edizioni turistiche

"VATICAN"
© LOZZI ROMA S.A.S.

ISBN 978-88-86843-30-0

Publisher:
LOZZI ROMA s.a.s.
Via Filippo Nicolai, 91
00136 Roma

Tel. (+39) 0635497051 - 0697841668
Fax (+39) 0635497074
Web site: www.gruppolozzi.it
E-mail: info@lozziroma.com

Printed by:
C.S.C. Grafica s.r.l. - Guidonia (Roma)
Web site: www.cscgrafica.it

Photographies:
Archivio fotografico Lozzi Roma s.a.s.
Archivio fotografico Fabbrica di San Pietro
Archivio fotografico Millenium
Archivio fotografico Musei e Gallerie Pontificie
Archivio fotografico Osservatore Romano
Archivio fotografico Scala

"VATICAN" IS AVAILABLE IN THE FOLLOWING LANGUAGES:
English, Italian, French, German, Spanish, Japanese, Polish, Portuguese, Russian.

Made in Italy

INDEX

INTRODUCTION

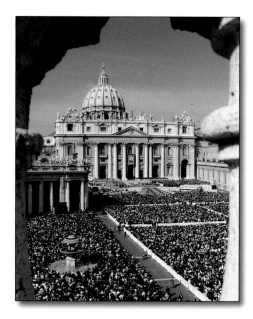

St Peter's Square thronged with the faithful visiting Rome from all over the world for the Pope's traditional Easter Blessing.

When in 67 AD an unknown centurion led the squad that was to crucify Simon Peter up the Vatican Hill, he could certainly not have imagined that he was laying the foundations of the smallest State in the world with regard to size, and the largest with regard to spiritual power.

The body of the first Successor of Christ was buried in that very place and about three centuries later, on this spot, the Emperor Constantine built a grandiose basilica, with five naves and a façade adorned with rich mosaics preceded by a broad atrium, which served as the model for the oldest Christian basilicas.

The Constantinian Basilica stood for more than a millennium, periodically reinforced by large-scale restorations. At the end of the 15th century, despite constant care, the ancient edifice seemed to be on the point of collapsing. There were plans to substantially rebuild it but nothing was done until the energetic and determined Julius II became Pope in 1503. The old church was then demolished and soon after (1506) work begun on the building of the new basilica which became the pride of Renaissance and Baroque Rome. It was a dreadful and fascinating spectacle: as if in the grip of a mania for destruction, Donato Bramante, the architect commissioned by Julius II to undertake this huge project, left not a stone of the old building standing. However Bramante was unable to do more than lay the foundations of the new building: he died in 1514, when the work was partly begun. The most important artists in Rome in the 15th and 16th centuries succeeded him: Raphael, Giuliano and Antonio da Sangallo, Michelangelo, Della Porta, Maderno, Fontana and Bernini. The work was only completed in 1665, with the building of Gianlorenzo Bernini's famous colonnade.

In the centuries to come, the Basilica, architecturally complete, was constantly enriched by numerous works of art. But the frenzy for construction in the Vatican was far from being over: indeed, the popes of the 16th and 17th centuries continued to add new wings and enlarge the Vatican palaces, both because of the increasing demands of the Papal Court and the desire to display the priceless art collections as they deserved.

Vatican City became an independent state through the signing of the Lateran Treaty between the Church and the Italian State on 11 February 1929. Important work was then carried out to make this small state, encircled by the powerful walls built between the 15th and 16th centuries by Julius II, Paul II and Pius IV, completely self-sufficient, and the span of the walls erected by St. Leo IV as a defense against the Saracens' raids in the 9th century was increased.

For more than six centuries (since 1377) the Vatican has been the

papal residence; the Quirinal was added in the 17th century. Before the papal court moved to Avignon (1309-1377), the Lateran was the seat of the papacy. There have been 265 pontiffs on the Throne of St. Peter in uninterrupted succession. For 20 centuries the Catholic Church, whose temporal power the Vatican State embodies, has played a vital role in the world's history through different vicissitudes down the ages.

ST. PETER'S BASILICA TROUGH THE CENTURIES

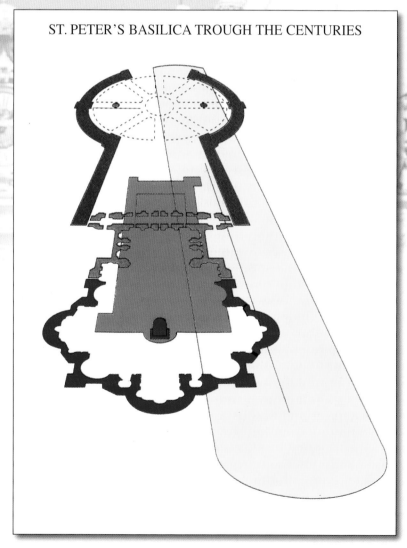

The diagram shows:
- In yellow, the ground plan of Nero's Circus (67 A.D.) on Vatican hill;
- In blue, the Constantinian Basilica (321 A.D.);
- In brown, the first part of St. Peter's Basilica built by Bramante and Michelangelo between 1506 and 1564. In the center, the tomb of St. Peter, next to the necropolis;
- In orange, the extension of the Basilica completed by Carlo Maderno in 1614;
- In green the Bernini's colonnade completed in 1667.

ST. PETER'S BASILICA

(The italic numerals in brackets, refer to the plan of the Basilica on page 96)

A portrait of St. Peter, Apostle of Christ and the Church's first Pontiff.

Very few nations in the world can boast a vestibule like St. Peter's Square. This extraordinary entrance gives visitors a sense of serenely profound balance, which may indeed be described as incomparable. The perfect harmony of the square with its colonnade and the basilica crowned by the famous dome makes it all seem like the work of one talented artist. Instead, the **colonnade** (1656-65) and its two curved arms were built by Gianlorenzo Bernini, one of the greatest architects of sixteenth-century Europe, about 50 years after the façade was finished by Carlo Maderno in 1614 and more than 70 years after the completion of the dome (1590). The pink granite **obelisk** standing at the centre of the square was made in Egypt during ancient Roman times. The fountain on the right was designed in 1613 by Carlo Maderno and the one on the left was designed in 1677 by Carlo Fontana. Though they were erected at different times, Bernini succeeded in perfectly harmonizing these many different elements. The artist worked on it from 1657 to 1665, declaring to have designed the colonnade as an architectural game of human body proportion. The colonnade's relationship to the basilica buildings is similar to the relationship of the arm and the head. Statistical facts: the colonnade has an ellipsoidal shape and it is made up of 284 columns arranged in four rows, interposed with 88 pilasters and crowned by a balustrade that holds 140 aligned statues of different saints created by Bernini's students.

Let us stop now and admire the **façade**: despite the massive horizontal breadth, which is conditioned by the size of the basilica, a sober nobility characterizes it. The *Loggia delle Benedizioni* (the central balcony) is where every new Pontiff is solemnly proclaimed.

An inscription in very large letters runs along the width of the façade, which celebrates Pope Paul V Borghese, who commissioned the architect Carlo Maderno.

Just as on the colonnade, the far balustrade has thirteen statues that are over three metres tall: the centre statue is the Redeemer, with eleven apostles and St. John the Baptist, the statues stretch out on both sides like wings. The twelfth is the head apostle St. Peter together with the apostle of the people St. Paul, and it is located down in the square on the side of the stairs to the basilica. From here, there is the access to the *portico* (n. 1), which is stately with vast dimensions: it is a masterpiece by Carlo Maderno. An important remnant of the Old Basilica is placed above the centre entrance: it is the famous *mosaic of the Navicella* (n. 2) attributed to Giotto (thirteenth century), portraying the boat of the Apostles in peril of sinking, with Christ and St. Peter walking on the waves. Even though the artistic value of this work is lessened by the various additions and retouches over the centuries, the work has great historic and testimonial value. In front of the railing

A fresco of the old Constantinian basilica.

Removing the Egyptian obelisk, which was later erected in Piazza San Pietro, from Nero's Circus.

The evocative atmosphere of St. Peter's Square in the Christmas season.

St. Peter's Square.

that encloses the portico are five large doors. They lead to the five aisles that divide the inside of the Basilica. The **main door** (n. 3), which was once located in the Basilica of Constantine is very interesting. It dates back to 1433, when it was completed by sculptor Filarete of Florence after twelve years of work. On the upper part, the *Redeemer* and the *Blessed Virgin* are both portrayed on the throne, while the four rectangles below portray *scenes from the lives of St. Peter and St. Paul*. The lively raised lines that frame the squares portray episodes from the Council of Florence, which temporarily ended the Orthodox schism (1439). The two doors beside the main door (as well as the door on the extreme left, are locked by bronze shutters made by contemporary artists. The first **door** (n. 4) by Giacomo Manzù shows death scenes. *The Death of Jesus* and *the Death of the Virgin Mary* are portrayed larger than the other scenes. One of the most distinct is the *Death of Pope John XXIII*, while *Death in the Space* has an extremely contemporary style.

The **Holy Door** (n. 5), which is located on the extreme right side of the Portico is quite interesting. It is only opened during the Jubilee Year, by the Pope himself, who then closes the door again at the end of the Jubilee Year.

From the atrium we move inside the Basilica: its well-known exalted size is not apparent at first sight, thanks to the careful study of the proportions of each detail. The visit starts from the *central aisle* (n. 6), which is flanked by three pairs of fluted *pilasters* with large arcades mounted on them. They cadence the vast barrel-vaulted ceiling decorated with coffers built in 1780 under Pope Pius VI. Near the central door, a grand *disc of porphyry* stands out on the rich marble pavement. In the old Constantine Basilica, it was located near the High Altar, and during Christmas night of the year 800, Emperor Charlemagne received the Imperial Crown from Pope Leo III while standing on it. On the interior face of the large pilaster, two series of niches open up with large statues. The lower ones represent the *founders of religious orders*, including St. Teresa, St. Vincent de Paul and St. Phillip Neri on the right and we can admire St. Peter of Alcantara, St. Camillo, St. Ignatius, St. Francis of Paola on the left.

The arcades as well, cadenced one after the other along the aisle, are decorated with allegorical *statues* that contribute to emphasizing the solemn devotional character of the overall atmosphere, while the interior faces of the pillars, covered with coloured marble, bear medallions with the figures of the first Popes. The *bronze statue of St. Peter* (n. 7), which was believed to have been made in the fifth century, stands out from all the sculptural decoration of the main aisle. More recent studies attribute the work to the twelfth century, most probably by Arnolfo di Cambio. The deep sense of devotion that it has evoked over the centuries is evidenced by the right foot of the statue, which has been worn away by the reverent kisses of the faithful.

The centre of the Basilica is right above the place where they venerated the Tomb of the Apostle two thousand years ago, a fact supported by archaeological discoveries. The *High Altar* (n. 8) is located beneath Bernini's grandiose canopy, and under the magnificent semi-spherical crown of Michelangelo's dome. According to the initial design by Michelangelo, the whole Basilica was supposed to have stretched out in a Greek cross plan from the main nucleus, with the length of the aisles equal in length to the arms of the transept. This idea highlighted the architectural unity of the whole and above all, the symbolic value of the central axis of the basilica which begins at the underground necropolis, passing through the main altar to reach the dome.

Despite the validity and severity of Michelangelo's project, under Paul V, Carlo Maderno finished the construction of the Basilica and worship exigencies brought about the decision to use a "Latin Cross" design with the aisles longer than the limbs of the transept, and therefore more spacious. The architectural and symbolic validity of the grandiose dome persists. It is firmly settled on four powerful angular *pillars*, in which Bernini opened four equally grandiose *niches* containing statues of Saints, which are colossal in size. The statues are representative of the relics contained inside the pillars themselves. The first pillar on the right shows the *statue of St. Longinus* (n. 9): it contains the *lance*, which according to the faithful, was the one used by the saint to pierce the chest of Jesus Christ on the cross inflicting

The Pope gives his traditional Sunday Blessing from his study window.

A typical view of the vast St. Peter's Square on a Sunday.

Saint Peter's grandiose façade by Carlo Maderno, crowned by Michelangelo's mighty dome.

Saint Peter's Square, bordered by the colonnade built by Bernini between 1656 and 1666. Its two arms are composed of 142 columns, in rows of four. 140 statues of saints, also designed by Bernini but made by his pupils, stand on the balustrade (below).

Opposite, the central nave of St. Peter's Basilica. Its vast dimensions are extraordinary: it is 46 meters high and from the entrance to the apse, 186 meters long.

The exterior of the Holy Door.

The Basilica's Holy Door from the inside.

The Door of Death by G. Manzù.

the final blow of mercy; the relic was placed there by Pope Innocence VIII.

The next pillar shows the *statue of St. Helen* (n. 10), who was the mother of the Emperor Constantine, and who faithfully searched out the Cross of Jesus. Urban VIII placed the precious relic, which came from the Sessorian Basilica, here.

The *statue of Veronica* (n. 11), is linked to one of the most touching scenes of the Via Crucis. According to religious history, the image of Christ's face remained indelibly printed on the linen cloth used by this pious woman to wipe the face of the Redeemer.

The fourth pillar shows the grandiose *statue of St. Andrew* (n. 12), whose head was carried from Acaia under the pontificate of Pius II and placed here together with the other relics, by Urban VIII.

It is the moment to look up above the powerful pillars to the dizzying height of the **Dome**. This is supported by four colossal spandrels that constitute the connecting elements between the quadrangular base and the circular bowl decorated with large circles (they have a diameter of 8 meters) in which the *Four Evangelists* are portrayed in mosaic.

The dome is subdivided by sixteen large ribs into sixteen slices, which harmoniously coincide with the huge windows beneath them. They are decorated with large *busts of the Sainted Popes and Doctors of the Church*, as well as other seated figures representing the Redeemer, the blessed Virgin, St. Joseph, St. John Baptist and other apostles; Above it are angels framed in four-sided figures alternated by seraphim heads in circular frames. Italian art has placed another splendid although extremely different interpretation of the solemn spirituality beneath the dome: the sumptuous *bronze baldachin* (n. 13). This is the first of the artworks in which Gianlorenzo Bernini applied his forceful idea of architecture to the Basilica.

The style of the canopy also characterizes the grandiose Cattedra Petri or "throne of St. Peter" that is also by Bernini, placed at the end of the apse, which we will look at later. The harmonic correspondence between Bernini's two masterpieces, which were built thirty years apart, should be noticed. Under the *Papal Altar*, reserved for the Pontiff, is the **Confessio** (n. 14), with two semicircular flights of stairs that go down to the level of the old Basilica of Constantine, built over the *Tomb of St. Peter*.

Going back towards the entrance of the Basilica, we will take the "external" path to discover the *lateral aisles*, the transept and the presbytery. Let's start with the aisle on the right which, exactly like the left aisle, contains various chapels.

In the first Chapel of the right aisle we are immediately touched at the sight of the famous **Pietà** (n. 15), sculpted by Michaelangelo when he was less than 25 years old. The deep pathos that animates the sculpture, portraying the eternally young Mother and her dead Son lying in her arms make an enduring image. This theme was felt

A picturesque view of the Vatican Basilica with the 16th century fountain designed by Carlo Fontana in the foreground.

On the left, the Baptismal Font.

The Holy water stoup is supported by gigantic cherubs (1725).

Michelangelo's Pietà - Details.

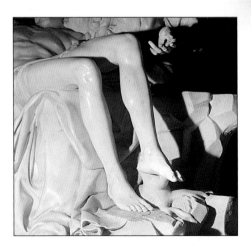

strongly by Michaelangelo, who repeated it many times in his later years reaching increasingly more spiritually satisfying results.

In the aisle, walking towards the transept, we find two important funeral monuments: against the first pier in the right aisle is a *monument dedicated to Christine of Sweden* (n. 16). After abdicating the throne in 1655, she converted to Catholicism, which is portrayed in the bas relief decorating the monument. She then moved to Rome acting as a patron of the arts for the culture of the city until her death in (1689).

In front of it we find a *monument dedicated to Pope Leo XII* (1823-1829) (n. 17). This monument is above the entrance to the elliptical Chapel of the Relics, which is open at the inside of the first lateral pilaster of the aisle. It is also referred to as the Chapel of the Crucifix due to the valuable medieval wooden masterpiece portraying Jesus on the Cross, which is attributed to Pietro Cavallini, a Roman artist of the twelve hundreds.

The next *Chapel of St. Sebastian* (n. 18) is named for the mosaic decorating it, which portrays the *Martyrdom of St. Sebastian*, taken from an altar-piece by Domenichino. At this point, we would like to remind visitors that almost all the paintings on wood or canvas used to decorate the Basilica, have been moved to the Vatican Museums or to the sacristies. Reproductions by the Vatican School of Mosaics have taken the place of the originals. In this Chapel, there is also a contemporary work: it is the *Monument to Pius XI* (1922-1939) (n. 19), made by Pietro Canonica in 1949, a decade after the Pope's death.

Another two funeral monuments follow: the seventeenth-century *sepulchre of Innocent XII* (n. 21) with a *monument to Countess Matilde of Canossa* (n. 22) in front of it, which is a masterpiece of both historic and artistic importance. The monument was designed more than five hundred years after the death of that paladin of the Church, by Gianlorenzo Bernini, while the statue of the Countess was sculpted by his student Andrea Bolgi. The work is reminiscent of others by the same artist that characterize many parts of the basilica, with energy and vitality.

A few steps away, on the right, is the vast *Chapel of the Blessed Sacrament* (n. 23) in which the Host is kept in a sumptuous gilded bronze *tabernacle* which was also designed by Gianlorenzo Bernini. Everything in the chapel dates to the sixteen hundreds: the large altarpiece behind the ciborium portrays the Holy Trinity by Pietro da Cortona. The mosaic on the right hand wall is from the Ecstasy of St. Francis by Domenichino. Francesco Borromini together with Bernini designed the gates in rod iron and bronze. At the time, Borromini, a protagonist of Baroque architecture, was a student of Bernini.

At last we have reached the *Gregorian Chapel* (n. 27) also called the *Chapel of Our Lady of Succour* named by Pope Gregory XIII. Beneath the altar, St. Gregory Nazianzeno, the Patriarch of Constantinople who lived during the second half of the fourth century, is venerated. The other name of the chapel is given by the small much-worshipped painting from the twelfth century, which came

Michelangelo's Pietà. ⇨

The bronze statue of St. Peter by Arnolfo di Cambio.
The tomb of St. Peter.

The Chapel of the Blessed Sacrament.
A solemn religious ceremony in St. Peter's Basilica.

Altar of the Falsehood.

Altar of the Sacred Heart.

from the old Basilica of Constantine, portraying *Our Lady of Succour* (n. 28).

Going back to the aisle, we admire, the *Communion of St. Jerome* (n. 29) on the angular pillar of the dome. This mosaic reproduction by Domenichino contributed more than any other, to the great fame of the artist.

We will move on to the *right wing of the Transept* (n. 32). In this ample area there are three altars: on the right is the *altar to St. Wenceslas* (n. 33) with the painting by Angelo Caroselli; in the centre the *altar of St. Processus and St. Martinianus* (n. 34) with the altar piece in mosaic reproducing the *Martyrdom of the two saints* from Giambologna's work. On the left, there is the *Altar of St. Erasmus* (n. 35), with a mosaic altarpiece from the sixteen hundreds, which represents the *Martyrdom of the Saint*, taken from a painting by the famous French painter Nicholas Poussin.

The large statues located in niches continue along the walls. Similar to those that line the main aisle, they represent the founding saints of religious orders. Passing by the second support pillar on the right, we find ourselves in front of another important artistic masterpiece, the *monument in memory of Clement XIII* (n. 36) by the great neo-classic sculptor Canova with sober elegance and considerable similarity to the spirit of his age.

Afterwards we visit the *Chapel of St. Michael* (n. 38), so called from the theme of the high altar-piece reproduced in mosaic. This work by Guido Reni from the sixteen hundreds portrays *St. Michael* and it sends forth a feeling of bold vitality. The fame of this and other works would earn the artist the nickname as the "painter of the angels."

In the next passageway we enter into the majestic apse (n. 42), its fulcrum is the scenographic **throne** of St. Peter (n. 43) with the unmistakeable signs of Bernini's artistic geniality. It is sustained by gigantic figures, measuring around 5 meters, of two fathers of the Latin Church, St. Augustine and St. Ambrose, and two fathers of the Greek Church, St. Athanasius and St. John Chrysosturn. The tiara and the keys, which are symbols of the papal authority, are supported by small angels, crowned by the throne of St. Peter epitomizing the symbolic value. At the back, a relief represents the fundamental evangelical moment in which Jesus entrusted his flock to St. Peter. Above it all is a round window full of light where a polychrome figure of the *Holy Ghost* shaped as a dove is surrounded by a phantasmagorical nimbus of glorifying angels.

On the right side we can see the *Monument in memory of Urban VIII* (n. 44), a work by Bernini. Despite the fact that it was realized more than twenty years before the creation of the throne of St. Peter, it shows one of the most significant merits of the artist, which was his ability to achieve a perfect balance between sculpture and architecture.

In front of it is a *Monument in memory of Paul III* (1534-1550) (n. 45) designed by Guglielmo della Porta. It was built a century earlier and placed here afterwards, to be set near the Urban VIII Monument.

The Chair of St. Peter, a theatrical work by Bernini. ⇨

Michelangelo's majestic dome.

The interior of the Michelangelo's dome decorated by Cavalier d'Arpino.

The altar of St Leo the Great with Alessandro Algardi's marble bas-relief.

The statue of Innocent VIII by Pollaiolo.

From the apse, through a passageway where you can view the *Monument in memory of Alexander VIII* (1689-1691) (n. 46), we arrive at the *Chapel of the Column* (n. 48), which is in front of the *Chapel of St. Michael*. The chapel takes its name from a piece of column, which came from the Old Basilica of Constantine, with a painted image of the *Blessed Virgin* (n. 49), placed on an Altar. On the right is a singular marble altar relief by Alessandro Algardi, representing the *encounter between St. Leo the Great and Attila* (n. 50). It is one of the main monuments of the Christian Middle Ages: the great pope, whose remains are kept in the altar below, managed to stop the powerful king of the Huns, saving Rome from invasion (452).

The *left wing of the transept* (n. 53) similarly to the right one, has three altars: on the right, is the one crowned by the mosaic altar-piece representing the *Incredulity of St. Thomas* (n. 54) by neo-classic painter Vincenzo Camuccini; in the centre is the altar dedicated to *St. Simon and St. Jude*, which also contains their Relics, with the mosaic portraying *St. Joseph* (n. 55), by Achille Funi. On the left, the altar is crowned by the *Crucifixion of St. Peter* (n. 56) taken from the baroque painting by Guido Reni.

In the passageway that brings us to the left aisle beneath the icy neo-classical work by Pietro Tenerani is the *Pius VIII Monument* (1829-1830) (n. 57) and there is the door that leads to the Sacristies and to the Treasury of St. Peter.

In the *left aisle*, we find the grand *Clementine Chapel* or the *Chapel of St. Gregory the Great* (n. 59). Its first name is for Pope Clement VIII, under whom it was built by Giacomo della Porta. The main altar, in which the *remains of St. Gregory the Great* (n. 60) are venerated (giving rise to the second name of the chapel), is topped by the altar piece in mosaic representing a painting by Andrea Sacchi portraying The Miracle of the Corporal undertaken by the Holy Pontiff himself (590-604). On the left wall of the Chapel is a *Monument to Pius VII* (1820-1823) (n. 61), which is by Danish sculptor Alberto Thorvaldsen, who is Roman by adoption and the first protestant to work inside the Vatican basilica.

Going back to the aisle, we admire the mosaic reproduction of one of the masterpieces of Italian Renaissance; the original is displayed at the Vatican Picture-Gallery: The *Transfiguration* (n. 62) that Raphael was unable to complete because of his death.

The passage that moves us toward the next Chapel shows, on the right, the *Monument in memory of Leo XI* (1605) (n. 63) by Alessandro Algardi. In front of it is a *Monument in honour of Innocent XI* (1676-1689) (n. 64) in which the French sculptor Pietro Stefano Monnot shows clear traces of the very acute and cultured Classicism of his country.

We now admire the *Choir Chapel* (n. 65), which together with the Chapel of the Blessed Sacrament, which it is placed in front of, in the right aisle, is the largest in the Basilica. It was built on a design by Giacomo Della Porta, one of the continuers of Michelangelo's dome.

The chapel owes its name to the wooden benches lining the two sides; the Canons of the Vatican chapter meet there to celebrate the Divine Office. The altar-piece portrays the *Immaculate Conception* (n. 66), taken from the original by Pietro Bianchi, while the ceiling is decorated with precious golden stuccoes. In the passage on the aisle, are two monuments built at very different times: on the right there is one of the few works of the twentieth century that have been placed in St. Peter's Basilica, the *Monument in memory of Pius X* (1903-1922) (n. 67), built in 1923 on a design by architect Florestano Di Fausto. In front of it is an artistic jewel of the Basilica: the *Monument in memory of Innocent VIII* (1484-1492) (n. 68) by Antonio del Pollaiolo, which once stood in the old Basilica.

The *Chapel of the Presentation* (n. 69) is named for the altar-piece on the main altar, the *Presentation of Mary at the Temple*, taken from the painting by Giovanni Romanelli from the sixteen hundreds. Many believers are touched at the sight of the incorrupt *body of Pius X* kept in the crystal and gilded bronze sarcophagus underneath the altar.

On the right wall is a magnificent bronze relief by contemporary sculptor Emilio Greco, representing *Pope John XXIII visiting the prisoners* (n. 70). On the left is the *Benedict XV Monument* (1914-1922) (n. 71), by Pietro Canonica.

The next passage in the aisle shows us the *Monument to Maria*

Tomb of Paul III.

Tomb of Urban VIII.

Mosaic reproduction of the Communion of St. Jerome. The original by Domenichino is in the Vatican Picture Gallery.

Treasury of St. Peter's. The Cross of Justinian II dates from the 6th century.

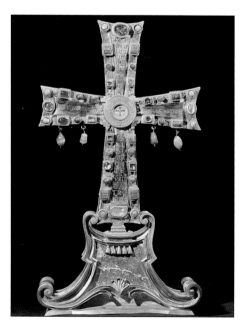

Clementina Sobieski (1702-1735) (n. 72) by Pietro Bracci illustrating the typical elegance of the seventeen hundreds. Across from it is one of the masterpieces by Antonio Canova, the marvellous funeral stele of the late Stuarts (n. 73), one of the last Catholic noble families in England. At the base of the truncated pyramid are two winged angels that rest on the torches of life, which are upside down and no longer burning.

Our last leg inside the Basilica is at the *Chapel of the Baptistery* (n. 74). At the centre is the Baptismal Font made of red porphyry from the classic age, completed in the seventeen hundreds by Carlo Fontana with a bronze rococò composition, rich in volutes and cherubs, culminating in the figure of the *Agnus Dei*. In character with the destined use of the Chapel, one of the altarpieces portrays the *Baptism of Christ*. The work is by Carlo Maratta, who was head of the Roman school between the sixteen and seventeen hundreds.

SACRISTIES AND TREASURY OF ST. PETER'S

At the end of our visit to the Basilica, let's return up the left aisle to the tomb of Pius VIII, under which there is the entrance to the *Sacristies* (n. 57). It is a series of rooms located in a small independent building attached to the body of the Basilica by two arches across the street. On the right of the entrance, is a list of the Popes buried in St. Peter's, since from St. Peter, the Prince of the Apostles.

A hallway leads to the *main or public Sacristy* built on an octagonal plan embellished with eight columns from the sumptuous Villa of the Roman Emperor Hadrian (second century A.C.) near Tivoli.

Among the adjacent rooms we highlight the Chapel that opens on the *Sacristy of the Chierici Beneficiati*, with the ciborium by Donatello, the great Florentine sculptor, who at the dawn of the fourteen hundreds was one of the promoters of the Italian and European Renaissance. It also contains the venerated image of the *Madonna della Febbre (Our Lady of the Fever)* by Lippo Memmi, a painter from Siena in the thirteen hundreds. Both the works decorated the pre-existing Old Basilica of Constantine. The chapel also hosts the plaster cast of Michelangelo's Pieta, which was a treasure in restoring the sculpture after an attack of vandalism in 1972.

The chapel is included in the halls in which the museum of the *Treasury* of St. Peter's is contained. There are many precious objects on display which remain from the incredible quantity of gifts and artworks received over the course of the centuries by the Holy See from all over the world.

Since the times of Constantine (fourth century) St. Peter's Basilica has received large donations. Over the course of the centuries, the Treasury was filled and enriched piece by piece. However, due to the fact that it was pillaged many times up until the Napoleonic era, the precious objects displayed date to the past two centuries for the most part.

The tomb of Sixtus IV by Pollaiolo is one of the rare masterpieces from the earlier Constantinian Basilica.

The *first room* displays the vine-covered column from the chapel of the Pieta and the rooster in gilded bronze from the ninth century, which adorned the bell tower of the old basilica.

The *second room* holds the *Crux Vaticana*, a cross in leather, silver and precious stones containing fragments of the real Cross; the *Dalmatic* (a liturgical vestment), which is said to have belonged to Charlemagne, but in reality it dates back to the eleventh or possibly the fourteenth century and many precious reliquaries.

In the *third room* is the striking bronze funerary *monument of Sixtus IV* (1471-84), a masterpiece by Antonio del Pollaiolo.

In the *fourth room* you can view the fourteenth-century *frame of Veronica* which used to hold the precious relic of the saint.

In the *fifth room* we see antique *copper spheres* used as hand-warmers in the chilly sacristies, as well as a collection of *precious chalices and reliquaries*.

Room six contains a vast collection of *candelabras*. The small room of the passageway contains large sacred codices. *Room seven* hosts a model of one of the *worshipping angels*, made in clay and cast in bronze by Bernini for the Chapel of the Sacrament. *Room eight* displays a collection of vestments, furnishings and votive jewels donated to the pontiffs by the faithful from all over the world. *Room nine* contains an example of paleo-Christian sculpture, the *sarcophagus of Junius Bassus* (4th century).

St. Peter's treasury. A precious Chalice studded with gems.

Mosaic from the Constantinian Basilica. Detail of St. Peter preaching to the Romans.

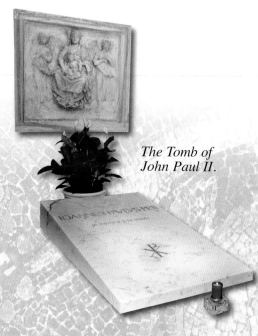

The Tomb of John Paul II.

Detail of a mosaic portraying a swan, the symbol of love, pecking at a pineapple.

THE SACRED GROTTOES

To visit the impressive remains of the old basilica built in the age of Constantine which stood for about 1,200 years, one must go underground. In the course of rebuilding the basilica, an effort was made to leave the ground-plan as intact as possible by constructing the new basilica on a higher level. Consequently, the existing subterranean passages correspond to the ancient building, with a slight difference in level.

The entrance to the **Vatican Grottoes** is found outside the Basilica, next to the entrance to the Cupola on the right side of the portico. The complex consists of two separate parts. The *New Grottoes* correspond to the transept above, and they are the starting point for ambulatory rays that lead to the four oratories dedicated to the same saints as the corresponding pillars, which support the dome, and three additional chapels. Beneath the central aisle are the so-called *Old Grottoes*, a large space likewise divided into aisles by two long rows of low, powerful pilasters.

Along the walls and between the vast pilasters separating the three aisles, are a series of tombs of popes, and of cardinals, bishops, kings and queens, while at the end of the aisles are some precious works of art. The last pontiff buried here (April 2005), John Paul II, took the place previously occupied by John XXIII, who was transferred to St. Peter's basilica, under the altar of St. Jerome.

In the centre of the galleria is the St. Peter or *Clementine Chapel*, whose precious malachite altar houses the ancient, unpretentious masonry altar, built by St. Gregory the Great (590-604) to "celebrate the Holy Mass on the body of the Blessed Peter" where the tomb of the apostle was indicated as being located since the first centuries. Important archaeological excavations of the underlying necropolis in the 1950s and 60s have confirmed this ancient tradition. The chapel has a singular "upside-down cross" shape, in memory of the martyring of St. Peter on a cross in the same position. Across this chapel is a simple shrine with the *tomb of Pius XII* (1939-1958), set as close as possible to the first Vicar of Christ in accordance with the pope's own wishes.

The kneeling *statue of Pius VI* has been transferred to the end of the main aisle. This work by Antonio Canova was completed by Adam Tadolini (1822) and it formerly stood on the level of the Confessio but has been transferred to the end of the central aisle. At the end of the side aisles are funeral monuments and sarcophagi of great historical and artistic importance: the *tomb of the Emperor Otto II*, a paleo-Christian sarcophagus and the *tomb of Nicholas III*, from the fourth century.

The exit from the Grottoes is located near the ticket office for the visit to the dome.

THE VISIT TO THE DOME

The entrance to the dome is located to the right of the portico of the basilica. After taking the elevator part of the way to the height of the central aisle (about 45 meters), we continue up to the vast terrace above the aisle itself. The massive dome soars to a height of 92 meters, surrounded by a series of 10 lesser domes. The view from the terrace is enchanting and picturesque, but nothing could be more amazing than the spreading panorama beneath the parapet with a view of the city marked by the winding ribbon of the Tiber.

From the base of the dome the subsequent and even more interesting phase of the ascent begins. First of all we will pause to observe the interiors of the Basilica from the height of the balcony encircling the first interior entablature of the dome beneath the large windows. While the colossal works we admired seemed real like miniatures from the ground; from here, the figures of the saints and angels decorating the dome look gigantic.

The climb continues up steps and winding staircases of different gradients and sizes squeezed between impressively curving walls, to finally reach the loggia around the lantern from which we can admire a second and even more extensive view of the city.

From the dome there is a 360 degree panoramic view. In the foreground the embracing curves of Bernini's colonnade can be seen. (From the dome itself, behind the Basilica looking west, the visitor has a complete view of the Vatican Gardens and palaces).

St Peter's Square at dawn ⤳

The modern spiral ramp which gives access to the Vatican Museums.

THE APOSTOLIC PALACE

The complex of Vatican palaces which extend from Saint Peter's Square to the wall of Porta Angelica can be divided into two sections: the actual *Apostolic Palace* where the Pope lives, and the buildings which currently house the Vatican museums. The two parts are adjoining so that they intersect at some points.

The *Apostolic Palace* can be visited only on the occasion of the Holy Father's private audiences, with a permit duly issued by the Prefecture of the Papal Household. It is entered through the *Bronze Door* which opens onto Saint Peter's Square, at the end of the right wing of the portico. From here a long corridor leads to the foot of the *Royal Stairway* designed by Gianlorenzo Bernini, which passes through the *Constantine Portico*. This is no more than the continuation of the basilica's atrium from which it is only separated by a door opposite the *equestrian statue of Constantine*, also the work of Bernini. The steps lead to the *Sala Regia* (Royal Hall) which Paul II commissioned Antonio da Sangallo to build.

The upper half of the walls in the *Sala Regia* is decorated with frescoes showing the activities of certain popes and is the work of painters mainly belonging to the "Mannerist" school which followed the great flourishing of the Italian Renaissance.

Next to the Sala Regia is the entrance to the *Pauline Chapel*, usually closed to the public. It is decorated by two famous frescoes by Michelangelo, the *Conversion of Saint Paul* and the *Crucifixion of Saint Peter*. The artist, commissioned by Paul II after whom the chapel is named, worked on these grandiose scenes between 1534 and 1550 when he was already getting on in years, after he had completed the apocalyptic Last Judgement in the Sistine Chapel.

Next comes the *Ducal Room* by Gianlorenzo Bernini; when groups were numerous, the Holy Father's public audiences normally used to take place here, in the sala Regia or in the adjacent *Hall of Good*.

In other cases, visitors were and are received in the sala Clementina as well as the *Consistory Hall*, or for official visits of important personalities, even in the papal apartments.

The *Clementine Room*, called after Clement VIII (1592-1605), is decorated with many frescoes including the remarkable great scene of *Saint Clement thrown into the sea*, painted by the Flemish artist Paul Bril.

On the right of this fresco is the entrance to the Papal Apartments, with eleven great rooms constantly supervised by the Swiss Guards. The *Throne Room*, exactly in the middle of the long suite, is suitably majestic; less grand but equally solemn is the *Small Throne Room* that leads into the *Holy Father's Study*, where the Head of Christendom carries out his daily work.

The cortile della Pigna. In the foreground the "Sphere within the sphere" by A. Pomodoro, set in the center of the courtyard in 1990. In the background, in the large niche by Pirro Ligorio, is the bronze pine cone which once stood in the Constantinian Basilica.

The spiral ramp (Vatican Museums), de-signed by Giuseppe Momo in 1932.

THE VATICAN MUSEUMS

The Braccio Nuovo built by Raphael Stern (1817-1822).

The Vatican Palaces are really a cluster of buildings whose construction began in the Middle Ages and continued under the auspices of numerous popes. The entrance to the museums is in the northern part of the external section of the Vatican walls. The portal on the Viale Vaticano, 10 meters high, is impressive. It is carved into the massive wall which marks the boundaries of Vatican City State and at the same time, props up the hill. For the Jubilee celebration in 2000 the Vatican Museums inaugurated a new entrance that substituted the monumental entryway that had been used in the past with a helicoidal ramp that was designed by Giuseppe Momo in 1932 which is currently used as the exit of the museums. The current entrance, which was praised by Pope John Paul II during his speech for its inaguration, has a modern helicoidal ramp that is slightly inclined connecting the entrance level with the Courtyard of the "Carrozze" which has been significantly redesigned. In the atrium are many artworks such as the polychrome mosaic which dates back to the 1st century BC and two contemporary works of art: the entrance doorway by Ceco Bonanotte and a sculpture by Giuliano Vangi.

EGYPTIAN GREGORIAN MUSEUM

The *Egyptian Gregorian Museum* faces the hemicycle (semicircular structure) in the *courtyard of the Pine cone,* founded by Gregory XVI (1831-1846) and was completely rearranged in 1989, according to modern museum criteria. The valuable exhibits are displayed in nine rooms; the *first room* contains *inscriptions and epigraphs*; the *second room* documents the *funerary cult*; in the *third room* are sculpted *figures from the Canopos Serapeum* of Hadrian's Villa in Tivoli; in the *fourth and fifth rooms* are examples showing the interesting relationship between Egyptian and Roman statuary. In the *sixth and seventh rooms* the *Grassi and Bronzetti collection* is on view; the *eighth room* contains a *collection of vases and ceramics*; lastly, the *ninth room* exhibits *reliefs* from the Assyrian royal villas of Ninive and Nimrud (9th-10th centuries BC).

The Gallery of the Candelabra is divided into six sections of arcades with columns and pilasters.

CHIARAMONTI MUSEUM

Access to this museum, either directly or through the Egyptian Museum, is from the beautiful *courtyard of the Pine cone* one of the three sections of the enormous courtyard of the Belvedere designed by Bramante. The Chiaramonti Museum is called after Pius VII (1800-1823) of the Chiaramonti family; eager to continue the work of his predecessors Clement XIV and Pius VI, he arranged for a large part of the Vatican collections to be housed here. He therefore had Antonio Canova design a long corridor flanking the cortile della

The Augustus of Prima Porta statue, which dates from between 14 and 29 AD.

Pigna, to contain about 800 sculptures. In addition to this great corridor, called the *Chiaramonti Gallery*, and the adjacent *Lapidary Gallery*, reserved for the use of scholars, the *New Wing* which transversely links these galleries with the parallel Vatican Library is also part of this museum. The impressive quantity of statues contained in the Chiaramonti gallery makes it impossible to describe them in detail. They are mainly *statues of divinities*, *busts of sovereigns* or *allegorical figures*, arranged in 60 sections bordered by pilasters.

The **Braccio nuovo** is a gallery 70 meters long, bordered by numerous niches and widening into an apse in the center where an allegorical representation of the Nile has been placed, a copy of an Alexandrian original from the 1st to the 2nd centuries BC, discovered in 1513 near the Campo Marzio in the heart of Rome.

Among the other valuable statues in this section, we mention the most interesting of the Chiaramonti Museum, the *Augustus of Prima Porta*, named after the Roman neighborhood where it was found. The emperor is shown here in an attitude of regal domination, wearing armor finely decorated in relief. The whole figure exudes a sense of masterful resolution. We also point out the figure of an *Amazon*, a copy of an original by Polycletus, the great Greek sculptor of the 5th century BC who was a contemporary of Phidias.

Another important copy is that of the *Doryphorus* (spear-bearer) also by Polycletus, who established the "Kanon", that is, the ideal principles for perfect human proportions.

A Hellenistic statue representing the River Nile, a Roman work of the 2nd-1st century BC.

The Apoxyomenos, the athlete cleaning his sweat away, dates from the 1st century AD and is a Roman copy of a bronze work attributed to the Greek sculptor Lysippus, made in about 320 BC.

The famous Belvedere Apollo was the first work with which Julius II formed the nucleus of the Vatican Museums actual collection.

Perseus, a neoclassical work by Canova.

Hermes, a marble copy from the time of Hadrian.

PIO-CLEMENTINE MUSEUM

The Pio-Clementine Museum owes its name to Clement XIV (1769-1775) and his successor, Pius VI (1775-1799) who was responsible for its final arrangement. It consists of twelve rooms, containing mainly Roman sculptures including numerous copies of Greek originals. Access to the museum today is through the former entrance made by Clement XIV, on the opposite side to the entrance Pius VI had built later. After passing the entrance arch with the inscription "Museum Clementinum", immediately on the left the visitor can admire the famous *sarcophagus of Lucius Cornelius Scipio the Bearded* (consul in 298 BC), recovered from the tomb of the Scipios on the Appian Way.

Crossing a circular vestibule adorned with a precious funerary altar, the visitor reaches the **Cabinet of the Apoxyomenos** on the right, called after the famous *Apoxyomenos*, the athlete shown using a special instrument to scrape away the oil and sand with which he had covered himself. The statue is the only copy in existence of the Greek original by Lysippus, a supreme artist of the 4th century BC and a favorite of Alexander the Great.

The visitor then immediately finds himself in the **Octagonal Belvedere Courtyard**, not to be confused with the large Belvedere Courtyard that lies between the Library and the Lapidary Gallery. Small but with exquisite dimensions, it was designed in the form of a quadrilateral with rounded corners by Donato Bramante. It was only in 1775 that it was given the octagonal form which distinguishes it today, with the addition of the portico by Michelangelo Simonetti, the architect responsible for organizing this museum. Subsequently, beneath the portico surrounding the courtyard, Canova closed off four small areas known as gabinetti "cabinets" which house some of the Vatican Museums best known statues. These are: the **Cabinet of the Belvedere Apollo**, with a marble copy of the bronze 4th-century BC Apollo that came to light at the end of the 15th century and was set here by Julius II together with several other statues which formed the first nucleus of the Vatican Museums collection. Then the original fragments of reliefs that adorned the Parthenon are of great interest. The **Cabinet of the Laocoon** contains the celebrated group of *Laocoon* and his sons being strangled by sea serpents which could have been inspired by one of the most famous tales from Virgil's Aeneid. This is an original work by three sculptors from the island of Rhodes, Hagesander, Athenodorus and Polydorus, and dates to 100 BC. It was found in 1506 on the Esquiline Hill. The **Cabinet of the Hermes** displays the statue of *Hermes*, a copy of an original attributed by many to Praxiteles (4th century BC). It also contains a precious Greek original dating back to the 5th century BC, representing the head of Minerva. The **Cabinet of Perseus** contains three statues sculpted by Antonio Canova to replace three ancient statues depicting the same subjects

The Laocoon is an original Hellenistic work of the 1st century BC of immense artistic value.

Aerial view of the Vatican. The Vatican Palaces, which house the Museums, are visible on the right.

The Gallery of Maps.

that were taken to Paris in 1800 after the signing of the Treaty of Tolentino between Pius VI and Napoleon Bonaparte. They show *Perseus* and two wrestlers, *Kreugas and Damoxenos*, sculpted according to the neo-classical ideals and faithfully inspired by the great examples of Greco-Roman art.

Next is the *Room of the Animals*, filled with statues of various kinds of animals many of which were so drastically restored in the 18th-century. On the left of the entrance is the statue of *Meleager* and his dog, a copy of the famous Greek 4th-century BC original attributed to Skopas, one of the best known artists of that time. The floor is covered with three 2nd-century BC *mosaics* of animal figures, with arabesques and plant motifs.

Proceeding to the right, the visitor reaches the long *Gallery of the Statues*. Many of them are truly remarkable. We limit ourselves to pointing out the copies of two originals by Praxiteles, the greatest Greek sculptor of the 4th century BC, the *Apollo* called *Sauroktonos* because he is shown in the act of killing a lizard and a *Silenus*, respectively in the rows on the right and on the left on entering.

This room leads into the **Gallery of the Busts**, containing an interesting series of busts many of which are Roman originals. Indeed,

The Belvedere Torso, which dates from the 1st century BC.

The Venus Felix is a Roman sculpture dedicated to the Empress Faustina, the wife of Marcus Aurelius. It was inspired by the Praxiteles Venus (4th century BC).

The statue of Meleager is a 1st-century AD copy of a Greek original, probably by the famous Skopas who lived in the 4th century BC.

the Romans excelled at this type of sculpture. The group known as *Cato and Portia*, which dates to the first century BC and shows a Roman married couple, is famous. Also worthy of note are several of the emperors' busts, including that of *Octavian*, the future Augustus, portrayed as a young man.

Returning to the Gallery of the Statues, the visitor turns right down a passage adorned with a *bas-relief* from the funerary stele of a young athlete, a precious Greek original which dates to the 5th century BC. He then enters the *Cabinet of the Masks*, a small square room elegantly decorated with mosaic paving from Hadrian's sumptuous villa near Tivoli. Indeed, the mosaics represent *theatrical masks* and a delightful *countryside scene with animals*. Alternating with precious oriental alabaster columns, four niches carved in the walls hold some of the most admired female statues of antiquity: in the center is the *Venus of Cnidos*, a beautiful copy of a famous original by Praxiteles; to the left is an elegant group representing the *Three Graces*, a copy of an original which dates to the 2nd century BC; on the left is a small copy of the graceful 3rd-century BC *crouching Venus* by the Bythnian sculptor Doidalsas.

Leaving the Gallery of the Statues and once again crossing the Room of the Animals, the visitor reaches the *Room of the Muses* which owes its name to the statues of seven of these nine famous mythological figures, patronesses of the arts, exhibited here with the statue of their leader, the god *Apollo of the Muses*. The group set against the wall consists of Roman copies of 3rd century BC Greek originals from Tivoli. A large number of portraits of important personalities of ancient Greece, mostly in the form of "herms" (small columns ending in busts) is also displayed, including those of *Pericles*, the great lord of Athens of the 5th century BC, and the immortal philosophers *Socrates and Plato*. In the center is the well-known **Belvedere Torso**, a highly celebrated Hellenistic fragment dating to the 1st century BC, signed by the Athenian Apollonius and discovered at the end of the 15th century in Campo de' Fiori, Rome. It is seated on a lion skin; headless and limbless, (only the thighs remain), it nonetheless demonstrates an exceptional knowledge of anatomy and a vibrant feeling of life. The greatest Renaissance artists, starting with Michelangelo and Raphael, expressed deep admiration for this fragment which is thought to portray Hercules.

The *Round Room* follows. In the center is a vast monolithic porphyry basin, more than 4 meters in diameter. Among the large-size statues standing in the wall-niches, are the famous so-called *Barberini Hera*, a copy of a Greek original of the 5th century AD, the golden age of Hellenic sculpture and the important portrait of *Antinoüs*, the Emperor Hadrian's favorite, a Roman original of the 2nd century AD. The niches alternate with as many busts, including one of *Jupiter of Otricoli*, called after the place where it was found, a copy of a 4th-century BC original and one of *Hadrian*, from that Emperor's mausoleum (today Castel Sant'Angelo). The *Greek Cross Room* follows.

Here two majestic porphyry sarcophagi belonging to two eminent women of Constantine's family are on view: the *sarcophagus of St. Helen*, the Emperor's mother, decorated with scenes of battles between Roman horsemen and barbarians and busts of Constantine and the saint, and the *sarcophagus of Constantia*, the Emperor's daughter, adorned with cupids harvesting grapes among vine tendrils.

The Round Room designed by Simonetti.

The porphyry sarcophagus of St Helen, the Emperor Constantine's mother.

GREGORIAN ETRUSCAN MUSEUM

This is located on the upper floor and is called after Gregory XVI. It houses finds from the excavations in southern Etruria, carried out mainly in the 19th century, which were rearranged between 1992 and 1993. Worthy of note in *Room II*, is the entire content of the *Regolini-Galassi tomb*, called after those who discovered it in Cerveteri in 1836; the *Todi Mars*, a bronze made in the 5th century BC, in *Room III*; the remains of a frieze from the time of Pius IV *depicting mythological* and *allegorical scenes* in *Room IV*; the *Guglielmi collection* in *Room V*, *precious gold jewelry* in *Room VI*, *valuable terracottas* in *Room VII*; the *Roman Antiquarium* in *Room VIII*; the *Falcioni collection* in *Room IX*.

Leaving the Etruscan Museum, on the right of the stairway is the

The Todi Mars dates from the 5th century BC.

Room of the Biga, at the center of which the Biga, a kind of chariot, takes pride of place. It was restored at the end of the 18th century with the original pieces made in the first century AD. The missing pieces were replaced by perfect imitations. Various statues line the walls, including the most famous of all antiquity: *Myron's discobolos* (discus thrower).

Here the *Gallery of the Candelabra* begins. Its name derives from the many marble copies of candelabra of the Roman epoch. Moreover, most of the sarcophagi and statues exhibited here are also replicas of Greek originals made in the Roman age.

The *Gallery of Tapestries* follows. Formerly the famous *tapestries of the Acts of the Apostles*, made according to the design of some Raphael cartoons were exhibited here, but they are now on show in Room VIII of the Vatican Picture Gallery. They have been replaced by ten tapestries illustrating *scenes from the life of Jesus* and were made in Brussels after cartoons by the Italian school.

After the Gallery of Tapestries comes the bright and colorful *Gallery of Maps* where the walls are decorated with frescoes showing the regions of Italy. It is interesting to see how these were already historically identified at the time they were made, under the pontificate of Gregory XIII (1578-1580), using new technical and scientific instruments for the cartographic reliefs.

Etruscan vase in bucchero.

The Biga is a Roman sculpture of the 1st century AD, restored by the neoclassical sculptor Franzoni who made the horses and the wheels.

A Swiss guard on duty in the Raphael Loggias. This is the upper floor of the loggias. The lower floor was begun by Bramante and completed by Raphael who made this loggia and the peristyle with architraves between 1517 and 1519. Today it gives access to the Secretariat of State. It is not normally open to the public.

The Raphael's Rooms,
The fire in the Borgo (detail).

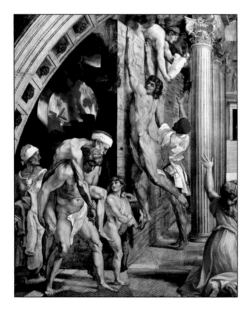

RAPHAEL ROOMS AND LOGGIAS

In 1508, while Michelangelo was beginning the decorations of the ceiling in the Sistine Chapel, Pope Julius II commissioned Raphael, who was still very young but already the idol of Patrician Rome, to cover the walls of the four vast rooms of his new residence with large frescoes.

The visit begins with the **Hall of Constantine**, reached through an external passage looking over the Belvedere Courtyard. This room is dedicated to the emperor who decreed freedom of worship for the Christians in 313. It was also the last to be painted, after the artist's death, so he had no hand in its decoration. There is even an ongoing debate as to whether the design for its decoration should be attributed to his pupils, Giulio Romano and Francesco Penni. The great scene of Battle of Constantine is attributed to the former.

From here, a door in the wall to the left of the *Battle of Constantine* leads to **Raphael's Loggias** which face the San Damaso Courtyard. They are not open to the public; we will therefore recall only their most essential features. The general concept of the decoration is attributed to Raphael, who planned a series of biblical scenes portrayed in panels above the small vaults of the arcades (the famous Bible of Raphael). The decorative cornice inspired by the Domus aurea (Nero's Golden House) is covered with stucco and ornamental motifs in fresco and the so-called "grotesques", interesting examples of artistic design which became widely popular at that time.

Access to the **Chapel of Nicholas V** is from the Hall of Constantine. It was adorned with frescoes by Beato Angelico (1448-1450) in which the master clearly narrates the stories of the two proto-martyrs Stephen and Lawrence, creating richly human scenes with great formal balance. Ornamental laurel leaves and flowers divide the frescoes on the walls into sequences on two levels.

The **Room of Heliodorus** follows. It was decorated between 1512 and 1514, by which time Raphael had completely mastered his technique. The room takes its name from the fresco on the wall of the entrance which depicts the *Expulsion of Heliodorus from the Temple in Jerusalem* for sacrilegiously attempting to steal the temple treasure. Flouting tradition, the main subject of the scene is not placed in the center but on the left side. The central section, empty in the foreground, seems to acquire an infinite dimension with its series of arches in rhythmic succession, amidst the play of light and shade. On the left, a crowd of spectators watches the dramatic scene; behind, superbly oblivious to what is going on around them, Julius II towers, seated on his gestatorial chair with a small group of papal dignitaries. Proceeding to the left, the visitor can admire the famous scene of the *Miracle of Bolsena*, masterfully arranged above a window. The episode illustrated took place in Bolsena in 1263: while a priest was celebrating Mass, tormented by doubts about the real presence of Christ in the consecrated host, he suddenly saw drops of blood dripping from it which stained the corporal. Julius II had a special veneration for this relic which is preserved in Orvieto Cathedral; so Raphael reproduced the scene and included the pope as an ideal witness.

On the wall opposite the entrance *Attila* (King of the Huns) *Turned Back from Rome is shown meeting St. Leo the Great.*

The fourth and last scene in the Room of Heliodorus is the *Deliverance of St. Peter from Prison.* Once again the artist has found a brilliant solution to the problem created by the presence of a window: in the lunette above, the apostle's cell penetrated by an angel shining with light is portrayed. In contrast, on either side the jailers lie on two flights of steps, stunned by the impact of the heavenly messenger's sudden appearance. The background on the left is lit by a gentle moon veiled in clouds which gives the scene a touch of pro-

The Raphael's Rooms, Deliverance of St. Peter from prison (detail).

The Chapel of Nicholas V is called after Pope Nicholas V Parentuccelli. It is located in the tower of Innocent III, one of the oldest monuments in the Vatican Palaces.
The frieze, painted in 1451, is the work of Beato Angelico and illustrates the histories of St. Stephen and St. Lawrence. On the star-spangled vault the four Evangelists are portrayed with their symbols.

The School of Athens is one of the most important celebrations of classical culture. Plato and Aristotle converse in the center of the scene. Below, on the extreme right, the face of Raphael himself can be recognized, staring out at the onlooker.

found melancholy. The decoration of the room is completed by the *biblical scenes* on the ceiling, attributed to Guglielmo di Marcillat, a well known 16th-century painter of stained-glass, and by the *mosaic paving*, an example of Roman art of the 2nd century AD.

The visitor then moves on into the **Room of the Segnatura**, so called because it was the meeting place of the ecclesiastical court of that name. This room was the first in which Raphael painted his frescoes, between 1509 and 1511, and it is particularly important because they are almost entirely the master's own work.

The *Disputation of the Blessed Sacrament* on the great wall opposite the entrance is a broad and serene composition, suffused with warm light. It all takes place on a double level: heaven, where Christ triumphant is seated against a background of an ethereal golden sky amidst his Apostles, while above, the Father giving his blessing rises majestic among angels poised in mid-air; and earth,

where a noble assembly of Fathers, Doctors of the Church, prelates and religious surround the altar surmounted by the Blessed Sacrament, the true protagonist of the scene and a visible link between heaven and earth.

The fresco above the window, to the left as one observes the Disputation, illustrates three of the cardinal virtues, *Fortitude*, *Prudence*, and *Temperance*; beneath, two monochromatic scenes (that is, of a single color) next to the window, represent the fourth cardinal virtue, *Justice*: on the left is the *Emperor Justinian delivering the Pandects* (civil laws) in the 6th century; on the right, *Pope Gregory IX approving the Decretals* that is, the codices of ecclesiastical law (8th century).

On the entrance wall, opposite the Disputation, is another vast masterpiece in which Raphael's art is visibly even more fluent and mature than in the preceding fresco: the *School of Athens*, a cele-

The Miracle of Bolsena, of indisputable pictorial value due to the three-dimensional representation of the figures and its vivid colors, refers to the event by which the feast of Corpus Domini (Body of the Lord) was instituted. We see Julius II himself portrayed kneeling at the altar, rivetted by the drop of blood appearing on the consecrated host, proof of the presence of the Body of Christ in the Eucharist.

Religious Modern Art Collection. Ecce Homo, by Georges Rouault (1946).

bration of human thought and knowledge. A vast, powerful basilica-like construction, inspired, it seems, by Bramante's project for St. Peter in the Vatican, is juxtaposed with an assembly of the greatest scholars and most learned philosophers of antiquity. In the center, Plato and Aristotle converse against the background of a great arch; in the upper left are Socrates and Alcibiades surrounded by their followers, and below, at the foot of the steps, Pythagoras is in the midst of a fervent group of musicians and mathematicians. The figure of the geometrician in the group (Archimedes or Euclid) who is tracing the drawing, has been recognized as Bramante. In the foreground, on the extreme right, Raphael himself is one of the two figures looking at the spectator, to be precise, the second. The first, in white, is held to be the famous painter Sodoma.

On the fourth and last wall on the right **Parnassus** is portrayed, the mythological mountain dedicated to Apollo and the nine Muses. Raphael solved the recurring problem of the presence of a window by integrating it in the view of Mount Parnassus. Apollo plays his viola in the center of the composition surrounded by the Muses and by the most famous poets of all ages, from classical antiquity to the painter's own contemporaries.

The next room is the **Room of the Fire in the Borgo**, the last to which Raphael contributed, painted between 1514 and 1517. In that period Raphael was at the peak of his activity: submerged by requests and not wishing to lose favor with the public, the master entrusted a large part of the execution of his work to his pupils, thereby lowering the technical and artistic standard of the works he had been commissioned to do.

The frescoes in this room show episodes whose protagonists are Pope Leo II and Pope Leo IV who lived in the 9th century; both are portrayed with the features of Leo X, during whose pontificate they were painted.

The most striking scene which has given the room its name is that of the *Fire in the Borgo*; it is the only one to have been entirely conceived by Raphael. Some episodes, certainly painted by the Urbinate (a native of Urbino, an epithet given to Raphael who came from that town), witness to the constantly high quality of his painting. The particularly evocative group of Aeneas, Anchises and Iulus on the extreme left are a clear allusion to the burning of Troy; the wonderful female figures of the "water-carriers" stand out on the right, and in the background, an echo of the old Constantinian Basilica which was already being demolished at that time.

Opposite: the Room of Heliodorus. The deliverance of St. Peter from Prison. The light shines from various sources and, dominating the darkness, gives color and form to the figures who appear in the three scenes portraying the event, as in a series of frames.

We will mention only some of the main frescoes in the room: on the right wall is the *Coronation of Charlemagne* by Leo III, a fresco attributed to Penni, with the assistance of Giulio Romano. On the left, is the *Naval Victory of Leo IV over the Saracens at Ostia* (849); on the window wall, the *Oath of Leo III*, by which the pontiff cleared himself of false accusations, in St. Peter's. It is attributed to Giulio Romano and by some, to Perin del Vaga.

Room of the Segnatura. The disputation of the Sacrament celebrates the triumph of the Church and the Christian faith. Raphael painted this fresco while he was still young, already displaying full and mature mastery of his artistic talent.

THE BORGIA APARTMENT

Beneath the Raphael Rooms and corresponding almost identically to their layout is the *Borgia Apartment*. It was built for Alexander VI Borgia (1492-1503) who had it decorated by the Umbrian painter Bernardino di Betto, known as Pinturicchio, and his school. After Alexander VI's death, his successor Julius II who had been bitterly hostile to him, had no wish to live in the apartment he had arranged; hence his decision to move to the upper floor, to the rooms decorated with the frescoes of Raphael and his school which have just been described.

The original purpose of the six rooms which make up this apartment is unknown. They have therefore acquired the names of the main subjects of their frescoes.

The *first room* is called after the *Sybils* who alternating with the Prophets are the subjects decorating the twelve lunettes.

In the *third room*, known as the *Room of the Creed*, are portrayed the *Apostles bearing parchment scrolls* on which the articles of the Creed are written. These first rooms are located in the *Borgia Tower*, a mighty edifice added by Alexander VI and recently restored.

The *fourth room* is called the *Room of the Liberal Arts* because of the frescoes glorifying the arts of the trivium (grammar, dialectics, rhetoric) and of the quadrivium (geometry, arithmetic, music and astronomy), on which the whole culture of the Middle Ages and the early Renaissance was based. The ornamentation of the ceiling is sumptuous, with frescoes, grotesques and gilded stuccos. This is the first room located in the wing built by Nicholas V; a few steps show the difference in level between the two buildings.

The *fifth room* contains biographies of numerous saints and is therefore known as the *Room of the Saints*. *St. Catherine of Alexandria disputing* is painted on a vast lunette opposite the window. In this scene, resplendent with light and color, is a masterful representation of Constantine's arch. Valuable 15th-century *Flemish tapestries* are hung on the lower part of the walls.

The *sixtht room* follows, known as the *Room of the Mysteries of the Faith*; it contains scenes in fresco that refer to Christianity's greatest mysteries. The *Annunciation*, the *Nativity*, the *Adoration of the Magi*, the *Resurrection* in which Alexander VI in adoration is shown on the left, clad in rich and sumptuous papal vestments, the *Ascension*, *Pentecost* and *Mary's Assumption into Heaven*.

The *seventh room* (the last), known as the *Room of the Pontiffs*, owes its name to the *portraits of the popes* that formerly adorned the ceiling and were lost when it was rebuilt.

The painted decoration of this room, the largest in the apartment, dates to a later period than that of the preceding rooms. It is the work of Giovanni da Udine and Pierin del Vaga of Raphael's school, and illustrates the important influence of this great master's art.

The rooms are adorned with fireplaces, ornamental pillars and furnishings of the age, which highlight their sumptuousness.

In 1973, Paul VI organized a large *collection of modern religious art* in the Borgia apartment and in a series of 55 additional rooms on the ground floor. He had an entire wing of the medieval palace rebuilt for this purpose, with large cross-vaulted rooms and many other smaller rooms.

The collection consists of about 800 works: paintings, sculptures and drawings, donated to the Vatican by more than 250 artists and collectors of all nationalities and tastes.

Borgia Apartment, Room of the Saints. St. Catherine of Alexandria's disputation with the Emperor Maximinus, by Pinturicchio - Detail.

Michelangelo, the Creation of Adam. Detail of the ceiling of the Sistine Chapel. The Creator transmits life to Adam through the contact of finger tips.

On page 56, three panels of Genesis. From the bottom: the Separation of Light and Darkness; the Creation of the Sun and the Moon; the Creation of Adam, the central scene of the cycle.

On page 57, a general view of the Sistine Chapel; in the background, the Last Judgement.

On pages 59, 60, 61, 62, a general view of the ceiling of the Sistine Chapel.

On pages 58 and 63, two lunettes of the cycle "The Ancestors of Christ", above the windows in the Sistine Chapel.

On page 64, a panel showing two scenes of Genesis: Original Sin and the Expulsion from the Garden of Eden (above); the Creation of Eve (below).

THE SISTINE CHAPEL

Between 1475 and 1483, Sixtus IV commissioned Giovanni de' Dolci to build the Sistine Chapel. He wanted this essential building to be architecturally isolated, virtually inaccessible from the exterior, as it were fortified.

Its decoration was begun in 1482 and it transformed the severe, almost bare chapel into a precious picture gallery of 15th- and 16th-century Italian Renaissance painting. It was Pope Sixtus IV himself who commissioned some of the best painters of the time such as Perugino, Botticelli, Ghirlandaio and Cosimo Rosselli to illustrate the parallel narratives of the Old and New Testaments which face one another on the central strip of both walls. The *Life of Moses* (Old Testament) on one side and the *Life of Christ* (New Testament) opposite, were therefore painted parallel to one another on the two lateral walls.

Thus *The Journey of Moses*, attributed to Pinturicchio, corresponds on the opposite side to the *Baptism of Jesus* which was certainly painted by Pinturicchio; in addition to the classical Christian symbolism, Roman monuments can be recognized on the hills in the background.

The next pictures are the work of Botticelli: the biblical series on the left includes *Moses with Jethro's daughters*, and in the Gospel sequence on the right, The *Temptation of Christ* and The *Healing of the Leper*.

Continuing, the *Crossing of the Red Sea* by Cosimo Rosselli, is an allegorical glorification of the great victory of the papal troops of Sixtus IV over the Neapolitans at Campomorte (1482), on the side dedicated to he Old Testament. Opposite is The *Calling of the first Apostles*, by Ghirlandaio, Michelangelo's master.

Next in the sequence on one side is *Moses receiving the Tablets of the Law*, which he broke after realizing that the people of Israel were dancing round the golden calf in adoration, and on the other, *The Sermon on the Mount*, both by Rosselli.

The biblical episode of *Korah, Dathan and Abiram* is another work by Botticelli, facing *The Delivery of the Keys to St. Peter*, painted by Perugino, Raphael's master.

On the left at the end of the series of frescoes on the lateral walls we find *The Testament and Death of Moses* by Luca Signorelli, while on the right is one of Cosimo Roselli's greatest works, *The Last Supper*.

In 1508, Julius II, ever eager for new enterprises, ordered the young Michelangelo to paint the **ceiling** of the Sistine Chapel. The gigantic work began in May 1508 and was completed on All Souls Day 1512.

The immense challenge posed by the vast size of the surface of the vault to be covered (an area of at least 800 square meters) and its

A religious ceremony in the Sistine Chapel with the Pope and cardinals.

IOSIAS

IECHONIAS

SALATHIEL

S·FABIANVS·ROMANVS·SE·AN·XIIII
M·XII·MARTIRIO·CORONA
TVR·AN·P·CCLXXVI·N   XV

S·LVCIVS·ROMANVS·SE·AN·
III·D·III·MAR·CORONATVR
X·P·CCLXXXII·M·VI·D·XIII

AZOR

SADOCH

PIO·X·PONT·MAX·
QVINQVAGESIMVM·
AB·INITO·SACERDOTIO·
ANNVM·AGENTI

INTPOLIVS·BAVARIAE·
REGNVM·IO·GENS·
HISCE·SPECVLARIA·
DONVM·DEDIT

IX·TVS·SECVNDVS·GRECVS·EX·AT
ENTIS·SEDIT·AN·II·M·X·D·III
MARTIRIO·COR·AN·XPI·CCCII·M

S·FELIX·ROMANVS·SE·AN·
IIII·M·IIII·D·XV·MARC·ORO
NATVR·AN·XPI·CCXIII·M·VI

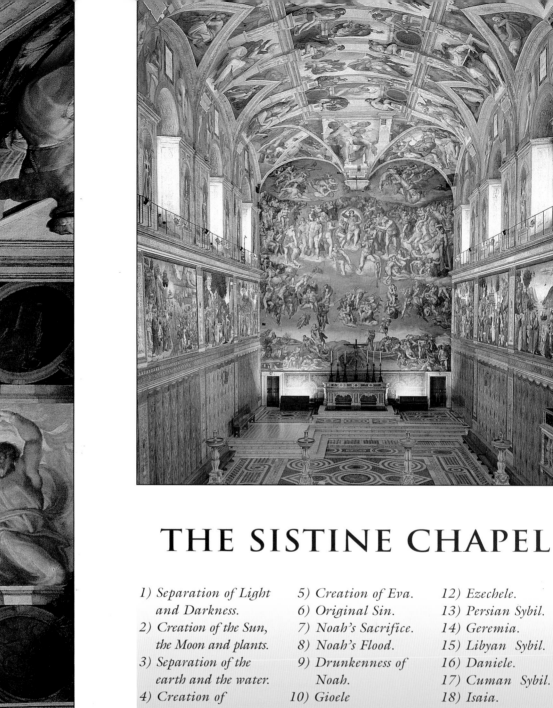

THE SISTINE CHAPEL

1) *Separation of Light and Darkness.*
2) *Creation of the Sun, the Moon and plants.*
3) *Separation of the earth and the water.*
4) *Creation of Adam.*
5) *Creation of Eva.*
6) *Original Sin.*
7) *Noah's Sacrifice.*
8) *Noah's Flood.*
9) *Drunkenness of Noah.*
10) *Gioele*
11) *Eritrean Sybil.*
12) *Ezechele.*
13) *Persian Sybil.*
14) *Geremia.*
15) *Libyan Sybil.*
16) *Daniele.*
17) *Cuman Sybil.*
18) *Isaia.*
19) *Delphic Sybil.*

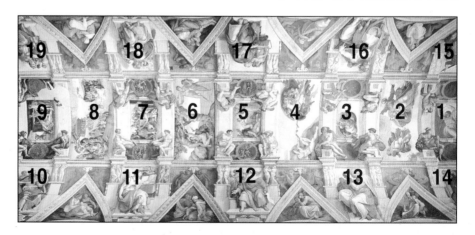

bareness was brilliantly overcome by Michelangelo with an inge-
nuity that reveals the rich complexity of his artistic genius. In fact,
he covered the actual architecture by painting over it an architectural structure in which he set the various figurative elements with
an amazing three-dimensional effect.

The artist incomparably combined painting, sculpture and architecture, making the most of the curves of the vault to fit his powerful figures into the scenes.

In the center of the complex design are a sequence of nine panels
showing Episodes from Genesis, from the main altar to the
entrance wall. They are flanked by the famous *ignudi* (nudes) and
portray respectively: the *Separation of Light and Darkness*, the
Creation of the Sun, the Moon and plants; the *Separation of the
earth and the water*; the *Creation of Adam*. This is the central
scene of the cycle, also from the pictorial point of view. The artist
expresses the sublime act of creation by the simple touch of finger
tips through which a real charge of vitality seems to flow from the
Creator to Adam. The *Creation of Eve* and the *Fall* follow original sin is a scene divided into two parts by the tree around which
is coiled the serpent with the bust of a woman; twisting to the left,
she invites Adam and Eve to pick the forbidden fruit. On the right,
cause and effect are visibly related in the drama of the expulsion
from the Garden of Eden. Outside the scene of earthly paradise, is
Noah's Sacrifice. This episodes celebrates his gratitude after sur-
viving the catastrophe and is chronologically later than the following scene of the Flood, a harmonious panel thronged with figures and episodes. Lastly, the *Drunkenness of Noah* ends the powerful sequence on the vault on a note of bitter pessimism about the
wretchedness of human nature.

The *Prophets and Sybils* between the triangular spaces at the curve
of the vault are the largest figures in this monumental work; they
are seated on solemn high-backed chairs and accompanied by
angels and cherubs. *Jesus' Forefathers* are shown in the lunettes
above the windows and in the triangular "spandrels", while the
four corner spandrels are painted with particularly dramatic
Episodes from the Old Testament, concerning the salvation of the
people of Israel.

A good 23 years passed, during which the Christian world was
torn apart by the Lutheran Reformation and Rome suffered the ter-
rible Sack of 1527, before Michelangelo painted the **Last
Judgement** on the wall behind the main altar. This unique masterpiece is overwhelming and dominated by the splendid audacity
of its author who put his whole self into it.

The Last Judgement, a compendium of the Divine Comedy and
the pictorial explosion of the "Dies irae", commissioned by Pope
Paul II, was begun by Michelangelo in 1535 and completed in
1541. Three hundred figures swarm in a composition which has an

*The Sistine Chapel. The Erithrean
Sybil (detail of the vault).*

The Sistine Chapel. The Prophet Isaiah (detail of the vault).

amazing coherence and clarity and in which space is organized into a real architectural structure of figures. Christ, the implacable judge, dominates this grandiose scene, his right arm raised in the act of condemnation. His words, "Depart from me, you cursed!" are not spoken, are not written, but they are tangibly felt. The Virgin beside him is the ever-living link between Christ and humanity. The other figures in the judgement are the prophets, apostles and the martyrs. On the Messiah's right are the elect; on his left, the damned.

Between the two lunettes, hosts of angels in heaven bring the symbols of the Passion. Below, on the left, is the scene of the resurrection of the dead: a group of angels in the center, bearing the Book of Judgement, blow trumpets, while the dead stir from gaping tombs to find themselves in the Valley of Jehoshaphat. As the good rise to heaven amidst the impotent rage of demons, the wicked are precipitated into the abysses where Charon shoves them out of his boat and Minos, the judge of hell awaits them.

Between 1980 and 1994 a large-scale restoration of the frescoes on the ceiling and the Last Judgement was carried out and attracted keen attention all over the world.

In fact, by dissolving the heavy layers of dust and lamp-black deposited on the painting with the passing of centuries and the clumsy attempts at restoration with animal glues in the 17th century, somewhat unexpectedly this in-depth cleansing brought the most brilliant colors to light, which has led some experts to revise the theory of the prevalence of drawing over the use of color in Michelangelo's painting.

THE VATICAN APOSTOLIC LIBRARY

The Library is divided into various sections: rooms, chapels, galleries and lastly, the Profane Museum.
The visitor first enters the *Room of Addresses of Pius IX* in the center of which the show-case displaying objects found in the excavations of Pompei in 1849 is of considerable interest.
Next to it is the circular *Chapel of St. Pius V*, whose form corresponds to that of two chapels located on the floors above and below. It contains objects from the treasury of the *Sancta Sanctorum*, the private chapel of the popes in the Lateran where important relics set in very valuable reliquaries were kept.
To the left of the chapel there is a collection of precious embroidered vestments. Through the door on the left on leaving the Chapel of St. Pius V, numerous examples of oriental Christian art objects can be admired.
The *Room of the Addresses of Leo XIII* (1878-1903) and *St. Pius X* (1903-14) follows, where many letters of congratulation to these popes are kept. Continuing from the Chapel of St. Pius V, a small

The Sistine Hall of the Library, commissioned by Sixtus V as a reading room. Many artists worked on its decoration under the direction of Cesare Nebbia.

One of the globes kept in the Vatican Apostolic Library.

room can be observed on the left of the Room of the Addresses: the extremely valuable Roman fresco of the *Aldobrandini Wedding*, one of the gems of the Vatican, is preserved here. This painting dates to the 1st century AD and was found on the Esquiline Hill at the beginning of the 17th century. It shows a wedding scene obviously inspired by a Greek work and executed with genius.

The long gallery continues with the *Room of the Papyruses*, so called because it contains a series of papyrus scrolls of the early Middle Ages (6th-9th centuries).

The next room, the Christian Museum, founded by Benedict XIV in 1756, exhibits important Christian antiquities including glass, bronze, silver and ivory objects from the Roman catacombs. There are also Byzantine and Oriental art works as well as early medieval objects, all of which merit careful attention.

This is in fact where the Library itself begins, with the Gallery of Urban VIII, which contains a collection of astronomical instruments. The two sections called the *Sistine Rooms* follow: on the dividing wall between the first and second room, on the side of the latter is a fresco portraying the *Transportation of the Obelisk to St. Peter's Square* (1586).

On the right of the gallery is the great salone Sistino *Sistine Hall*, the heart of the library, preceded by a vestibule. This is a vast room 70 meters long with two vaulted aisles supported by seven pilasters. It was built between 1587 and 1589 by Domenico Fontana on the orders of Pope Sixtus V, and it is decorated with *frescoes of Roman views* of that time.

The artistic splendor of the Sistine Hall should not make the visitor forget the value of the documents exhibited in the show-cases: *manuscripts* dating to the 4th century, *palimpsests*, or in other words, ancient parchments scratched out in the Middle Ages so that new texts could be written on them, incunabula or examples of the most *ancient printed books* and *drawings and miniatures* by expert artists. Lastly, one show-case contains a large variety of *papal coins* from different periods.

The visitor then proceeds to the sections of the corridor called the Pauline Rooms, designed during the pontificate of Paul V, that is, in the first two decades of the 17th century. Next is the *Alexandrine Room* (called after Alexander VIII) opposite the exit of the Braccio Nuovo, which was created in 1690.

The *Clementine Gallery* follows, it owes its name to Clement XII (1730-490). In a series of show-cases precious objects from classical antiquity are displayed, such as *cameos*, *reliefs*, *gold objects* and interesting documents including a decree of 260 AD, engraved on a bronze plate.

In the library's small *Profane Museum* which ends the long ambulatory of the Vatican Library, objects of Roman and Etruscan antiquity are exhibited, including *imperial portraits*, *bronze statuettes*, *mosaics*, and *carved ivory*.

THE VATICAN PICTURE GALLERY

The pictures exposed in the Vatican Picture Gallery are of exceptional interest: they are part of a collection begun by Pope Pius VI (1775-1799) which underwent various removals before being worthily housed in this functional building. Today the Picture Gallery contains about five hundred works between pictures and tapestries, arranged in the eighteen rooms which compose it according to chronological order: from the Byzantines and early Italians of 1100-1300, whose works are exposed in the 1st room, we arrive, in fact, to the artists of 1700 and the beginning of 1800. However, the nucleus of the collection is made up by the works of the greatest masters of the Italian Renaissance, of a really inestimable value. We shall limit ourselves to noting only the principal works exposed:

1st Room - **Early Italians and Byzantines** - A notable work is the *Last Judgment* of the Roman Benedictine school of the second half of the 12th century, on a tableau of a circular shape, the work of Giovanni and Niccolò. It is one of the most ancient known pictorial representations of the Last Judgment. Of great value also is the portrait of *St. Francis* at the bottom of which we find the signature of the author, Margaritone d'Arezzo, one of the first of the painters who signed their own works. Also worthy of note are some unique little

Filippo Lippi, The coronation of the Virgin.

The section of the Vatican Museums which houses the Vatican Picture Gallery built by Luca Beltrami in 1932.

The Coronation of the Virgin (1503), painted by Raphael before he was 20 years old, in which the influence of his master, Pietro Perugino can be seen.

pictures of 16th century Russian art, and a *Virgin and Child* by Vitale da Bologna, a painter of the second half of the 14th century, also called "Vitale of the Madonnas". In the middle of the room we find the so-called *Cope of Boniface VIII* of the XIIIth century.

2nd Room - **Giotto and followers** - At the centre dominates the *Polyptych* (that is, a large altar painting composed in several parts) called "Stefaneschi", from the name of the Cardinal who coimmissioned it from Giotto, who executed it with the assistance of some of his pupils. The work, recently recomposed, at the sides represents scenes from the lives of Sts. Peter and Paul, while at the centre is the solemn figure of the benedicting Redeemer, seated on the throne between two wings of angels and adored by the same Cardinal Stefaneschi, represented below to the left. On the estrade, below the three large scenes surmounted by three gables, is represented the Madonna on the throne with the Child, flanked by two Angels and the Twelve Apostles. The back of the Polyptych, it painted too, represents St. Peter on the throne at the centre, and at the sides the Apostles St. James, St. Paul, St. Mark and St. John.

3rd Room - **Beato Angelico** - Here are exposed some very small tableaux by this famous XVth century painter, among which are two episodes of the life of *St. Nicholas of Bari*, of an almost miniature nature, and the celebrated, most delicate *Virgin and Child*, among *Sts. Domenic, Catherine and Angels*, also this one is of tiny dimensions. On the splendid gilt background sprinkled with little roses, the figure of the Virgin stands out solemn and at the same time incorporeal. The affectionate attitude of the Child, the sweet eloquence of the glances binding Mother and Son, give to the scene a sense of warm humanity. The room furthermore presents three large polyptychos, among which the two interesting ones on the side walls: on the left the *Coronation of the Virgin* by Filippo Lippi, on the right the *Virgin handing the girdle to St. Thomas* by Benozzo Gozzoli, both influenced by Angelico's art.

4th Room - **Melozzo da Forlì** - This powerful 15th century painter knew how to give deep expression to his works of the "humanistic" character of his times, which was abstracted from the vivid and working admiration for classic antiquity. The room is dominated by the large fresco which the artist had executed in the Vatican Library, later removed and placed on canvas, in order to be better kept in the Picture Gallery rooms. It represents *Sixtus IV receiving the humanist Platina*, remarkable for the psychological acuteness of the portraits of the numerous retinue, and the harmonious sense of composition. Also unforgettable are the figures of the *musician Angels and the Apostles*, coming from the frescoed decoration of the ancient apse of the church of the Holy Apostles, demolished in the 18th century to make place for a larger apse. In the room there is also exposed a vast *Flemish tapestry* of the 16th century, reproducing the *Last Supper* by Leonardo da Vinci.

5th Room - **Minor painters of the 15th century** - Besides Italian

artists, the room also has Flemish, French and German painters.

6th Room - **15th century polyptychos** - There is a remarkable *Polyptych* by the Venetian Antonio Vivarini, which at the centre shows a singular St. Anthony Abbot in "alto-rilievo" of painted wood, surmounted by Christ suffering and surrounded by various Saints. There are also some individual pictures exposed in the room, among which the lovely Virgin and Child by the Venetian Carlo Crivelli, signed and dated.

7th Room - **15th century Umbrian School** - The room constitutes an interesting vestibule to the following room, entirely dedicated to Raphael: it presents, in fact, works of Umbrian artists, belonging to the same region as the great painter, some of whom are particularly tied to him. Here in fact is a painting by Perugino, Raphael's master: the *Virgin and Child and four Saints*, and a picture by Giovanni Santi, Raphael's father, representing *St. Jerome*.

Giotto, the Stefaneschi Polyptych. Painted by the great artist, with the help of many of his pupils for Cardinal Caetani Stefaneschi in about 1315. Tempera on wood.

The Transfiguration by Raphael.

St. Jerome by Leonardo da Vinci; an incomplete work by the great master which dates to the early 1480's.

8th Room - **Raphael** - The room houses three of the most famous paintings and ten tapestries of the great master from Urbino. On the large wall in front of the entrance we can admire the three great paintings. On the right is the *Coronation of the Virgin*, an early work of the artist, painted in 1503.

On the left is the *Foligno Madonna*, which Raphael executed in Rome in 1512, at the time of the greatest splendour of his art. The composition has become free and personal; a rich colour animates the scene, characterised by a perfect balance between Heaven and earth. At the centre, finally, is exposed the celebrated **Transfiguration**, which Raphael left unfinished at his sudden death which struck him down in 1520, at the age of only thirty-seven. The painting was exposed in the Sistine Chapel, before the deeply moved Romans, during the artist's funeral. It was later completed in the lower part, rather dark and agitated, in obvious contrast to the stupendous immateriality of the upper part, by Giulio Romano and Francesco Penni, two of Raphael's principal pupils.

9th Room - **Leonardo da Vinci** - The visitor is impressed by *St. Jerome* by Leonardo da Vinci, left unfortunately unfinished, like many, too many works of that genial artist, writer and scientist of the Renaissance, whose uneasy and multiform genius did not allow him to dedicate himself intensely to any activity. While on the landscape background some traces of colour are unfolded, the expressive figure of the Saint and the mighty lion nestling at his feet are only drawn on the canvas, prepared with an ochre-coloured ground. In front of this is a precious painting by another great artist who lived between the 15th and 16th centuries: the *Burial of Christ* by the Venetian Giovanni Bellini or "Giambellino", a painter considered by many as the greatest Venetian master of his times, who could mould his forms in colour, rather than model them with lines and "chiaroscuro", as had been done up to then.

10th Room - **Titian, Veronese and various 16th century artists** - The room is dominated by the immense *Madonna de' Frari*, a typical work of the most representative painter of Venice, Titian. During the long decades of his prodigious activity, the artist, who died when he was over ninety produced countless masterpieces. The Madonna de' Frari is one of these, for the wealth of its vivid and luminous colours, for the warm harmony pervading the scene, typical endowments of this great painter whom all consider a great Venetian, while in reality he was born in Pieve di Cadore. Beside this great canvas is *St. Helen* by Paolo Veronese, another great exponent of the 16th century Venetian painting, the author of bright and luminous pictures.

11th Room - **Muziano and Barocci** - Among the others as Ludovico Caracci, Giorgio Vasari, Cavalier d'Arpino, Girolamo Muziano and Federico Barocci stand out, both notable representatives of the Roman artistic circle.

12th Room - **Baroque painters** - This Room, of an octagonal shape, presents paintings of considerable dimensions of the most represen-

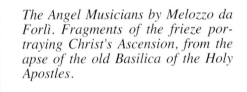

The Angel Musicians by Melozzo da Forlì. Fragments of the frieze portraying Christ's Ascension, from the apse of the old Basilica of the Holy Apostles.

Melozzo da Forlì. Sixtus IV and Platina.

tative figures of the 17th century. The visitor is struck above all by the *Deposition of Christ from the Cross* by Caravaggio although known through countless reproductions, the painting, seen directly, reveals a really magical luminosity which no reproduction, however perfect, could express. In that steady and sparkling light: the bodies appear carved like statues, and even the most natural and even vulgar details, for which the artist was bitterly criticised by his contemporaries, assume an aspect of incomparable nobility. Despite the lofty quality of the Caravaggio canvas, we cannot exempt ourselves from dwelling on other very estimable works exposed in the same room: the *Crucifixion of St. Peter*, placed to the right of the Caravaggio painting, the work of Guido Reni. Another very famous painting exposed in this Room is the *Communion of St. Jerome* by Domenichino, with a theatrically scenographic composition.

13th Room - **Painters of the 17th and 18th centuries** -We note *Saint Francis Xavier* painted by the Flemish artist Anton Van Dyck, who lived for a long time in Italy before going to London, where he became the painter to the Court of Charles I, contested

St. Matthew the Evangelist by Guido Reni (detail). The Apostle concentrates on writing the Gospel that an angel is dictating to him.

Vatican Picture Gallery - Raphael, the Madonna of Foligno.

by all the aristocracy. Here we found the great *Virgin and Child* by Carlo Maratta and two paintings of Peter of Cortona.

14th Room - **Painters of various nationalities of the 17th and 18th centuries**. Among others, it is worth noting the painting by Pierre-Paul Rubens, one of the greatest Dutch painters of the 17th century, who lived in Italy for eight years. It represents the *Glorification of Vincenzo l Gonzaga Duke of Mantova*, at whose service the artist worked during his stay in Italy. Very popular, finally, is the *Virgin and Child* by Sassoferrato, a painter clever above all in design.

15th Room - **Portraits from the 16th to the 19th centuries** - The portraits arranged in this room represent Popes, kings and illustrious people of those centuries. We shall mention the *Portrait of the Doge Marcello*, the work of Titian, of a pure and wise line; the elegant *Portrait of George V of England* by Sir Thomas Lawrence, the great 19th century English portrait painter, principal representative of the "Regency" style; the *Portrait of Clement IX*, the masterpiece of Carlo Maratta, in which are admirable the warm symphony in red of the colour and the psychological acuteness with which the Pontiff's face is represented.

16th, 17th, 18th Rooms - **Painters of the 19th and 20th centuries**, among them we remember paintings and sculptures work of modern artists as Rodin, Fazzini, Morandi, Carrà, Greco, Manzù and Villon.

Detail of the Communion of St. Jerome by Domenichino.

The fountain by Carlo Fontana with an evocative night view of Michelangelo's dome.

Funeral stele of a young athlete. Greek original from the 5th century BC.

Sophocles, a copy of the imperial age.

THE GREGORIAN MUSEUM OF PROFANE ART

The Gregorian Museum of Profane Art, founded by Gregory XVI in 1844 and today a rational modern structure that enables the works to be well displayed, offers the visitor an opportunity to wander between the original Greek collection, the Roman reproductions and imitations of Greek originals, Roman sculptures from the Republican period and from the first imperial ages, in addition to sarcophagi, urns and other later sculptures.

Among the many works, we mention those of major interest, such as the bronze group of *Athena and Marsyas* by Myron from the Acropolis, Athens; *three fragments of architectural decoration* by Phidias from the Parthenon in Athens, which date to the 5th century BC: a *horse's head*, which belonged to Athena's quadriga, the *head of a boy* and the *bearded head of Erectheus*.

In a neighboring room we can admire the *mosaic paving* known as the *Asaroton Mosaic*, a reproduction of a Hellenistic mosaic from Sosos in Pergamon made by Heracletus. Opposite, in another room, is the *Chiaramonti Niobide*, a copy probably inspired by the group of dying niobids attributed to Praxiteles or Skopas. In the *section of Roman sculpture from the 1st and 2nd centuries AD*, is the so called *Altar of the Vicomagistria* which dates to the 1st century A.D, portraying a sacrificial procession.

Also exhibited are the *Chancery reliefs* which illustrate interesting episodes of public life in Imperial Rome, buildings and mythological figures.

In the section of Roman sculpture of the 2nd and 3rd centuries AD is the *statue of Antinoüs*, the Emperor Hadrian's young favorite, another of *Aesculapius* and one of *Diana of Ephesus*.

The **Pio Christian Museum** was founded in 1854 by Pius IX; it contains material from the catacombs and the ancient Christian basilicas.

Missionary Museum of Ethnology (1926), contains countless sacred objects from all over the world.

The Vatican Museums also include the **Philatelic and Numismatic Museum** which occupies the upper floor of the Vatican Railway Station in Vatican City. The entrance is through the Arco delle Campane.

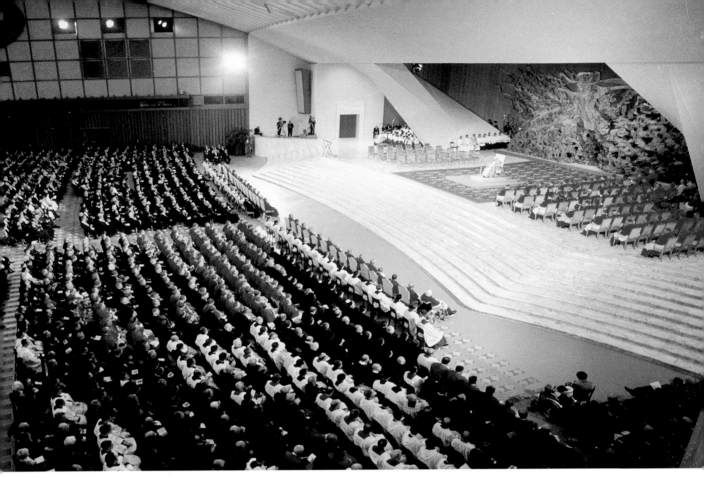

Above: a papal audience in the Paul VI Auditorium.   *Below: detail of Fazzini's sculpture.*

View of the dome of St. Peter's from the Vatican Hill, seen from the gardens.

INSIDE VATICAN CITY

To have at least a rough idea of the microcosm enclosed within the precinct of the Vatican walls, it is worth dedicating a few hours to visiting the interior of the Leonine city (access is only permitted for guided visits organized by the information office in St. Peter's Square, in the left wing of the parvis). The Vatican City State was established with the Lateran Treaty in 1929 which put an end to the dissent between the Church and the State that had dragged on for almost sixty years and began when Rome was taken by Italian troops in 1870. It occupies an area of 44 hectares (108.7 acres) and has a population of just over 1000 inhabitants and several thousand workmen, employees and officials who work but do not live in Vatican City.

They have the task of making the small but complete mechanism of the city function. It is equipped with a radio station, a railway station, four post offices, the editorial offices of the newspaper, the printing press, and workshops of an artistic kind including the famous School of Mosaics which is responsible for maintenance of

The relief on the pedestal of the column of Antoninus Pius, in the cortile delle Corazze.

The Palace of the Governorship, designed in 1928, houses the admni strative offices of Vatican City.

The Casina di Pio IV (small house of Pius IV) immersed in the greenery of the Vatican gardens. It was built between 1555 and 1560 by Pirro Ligorio, the architect of the splendid Villa d'Este in Tivoli.

The Fountain of Galleon.

Above: A view of the Casina di Pio IV.

The Fountain of the Eagle.

the mosaics of the basilica's altar-pieces and the tapestry workshop. Entering the Arco delle Campane, the visitor finds himself in the *largo dei Protomartiri Romani*, on the spot occupied in ancient times by part of the "spina" of Nero's Circus. A marble disk marks the point where the obelisk which today stands in the center of St. Peter's Square originally stood. Next to this area is the *largo della Sagrestia*, where the entrance to the Vatican Necropolis is located and which leads to the *piazza di Santa Marta*, the largest square in the Vatican from which there is an impressive view of the basilica's massive apse.

In the center of the square is a delightful little garden with a fountain overlooked by the *Domus Sanctae Martae* and the *palazzo San Carlo*, built on the spot where the house of Pierluigi da Palestrina once stood, as a stone tablet recalls. Beyond the piazza di Santa Marta on the left are the the *Vatican law courts* the *house of the Archpriest of the Vatican* the *School of Mosaics*, the solemn and sober railway station. Continuing to the right is the *Church of Santo Stefano of the Abyssinians* of most ancient origins. Indeed, it seems to have been founded in the 6th century; in later centuries various restorations have given it its current form.

The *Palace of the Governorship* is precisely perpendicular to the basilica. Behind this grandiose palace which houses the administrative offices that see to the functioning of the City's bureaucratic machinery, are the **Gardens** which extend as far as the boundary walls of the Vatican, creating a most pleasant oasis of greenery. Access to the gardens (where the Pope is in the habit of strolling) is permitted only to guided visits, with appropriate shuttle-buses. In the gardens are the Ethiopian College, the Radio Station, set on

The Fountain of the Mermaid, in the rose garden.

Swearing-in ceremony of the Swiss Guards in the San Damaso Courtyard.

the top of the Vatican hill, and the reconstructed Lourdes Grotto. The gardens are also scattered with numerous fountains, some of which have historical importance.

The Casina Pio IV (small house of Pius IV) stands in the midst of this greenery, close to the Vatican Museums. It is the work of the late-Renaissance architect, Piro Ligorio, and the seat of the Accademia dei Nuovi Lincei (today the Pontifical Academy of Sciences) whose members are scientists of various nationalities.

On the left of the *Arco delle Campane*, a vast area is occupied by the *Paul VI Auditorium*, for papal audiences, designed by Pierluigi Nervi and inaugurated in 1971. It is the Vatican's most recent architectural work. In addition to its extraordinary size - it has a capacity of 12,000 - its unusual architectural style dominated by a dynamic convex parabolic ceiling in the form of a shell is impressive. At the back of the hall, behind the papal podium, towers the grandiose *sculpture of the Resurrection* made in bronze and copper by Pericle Fazzini in 1976.

THE SWISS GUARDS

A Swiss Guard in dress uniform, whose design is traditionally attributed to Michelangelo.

The need to be able to rely on a small but trustworthy army spurred Pope Julius II to create the Swiss Guard Corps (*Cohors pedestris Helvetiorum a sacra custodia Pontificis*) in 1506. An agreement with the Helvetic Confederation guaranteed a supply of soldiers, all Catholics from the German-speaking cantons, ready to serve the Pope.

Since then, there have not been many changes in the criteria for their recruitment. Great pains are still taken in selecting them today, considering as indispensable prerequisites the moral reliability, physical integrity and aesthetic appearance of the recruits.

In their colourful uniforms with slashed sleeves and puffed knickerbockers designed in the 16th century, the Swiss Guards have been involved since that time in the history of the papal State.

They were formerly reinforced by the Noble Guard, recruited from among Rome's nobility, by the Palatine Guard, and by the Papal Police Force.

In 1970 Paul VI dismissed the armed papal guards but he retained the Swiss Guards who are still on duty at solemn liturgical celebrations and during celebrities' visits to the Pope and actively guard all the gates of access to Vatican City.

The Swiss Guard Corps staff is nowadays of one hundred men.

Parade of the Swiss Guards in Saint Peter's Square.

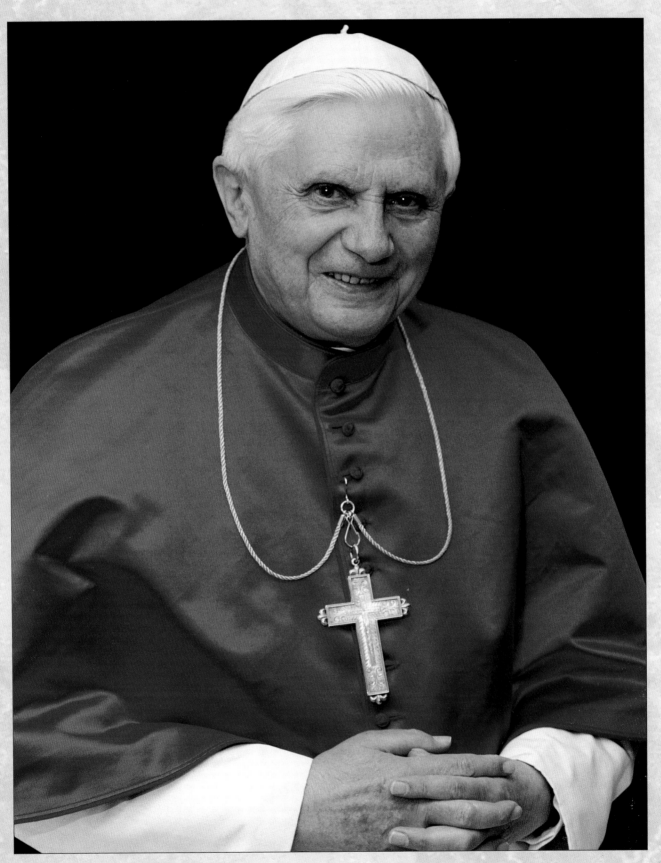

 Benedictus PP XVI

 Joannes Paulus PP. II

A SHORT HISTORY OF THE PAPACY

The title "Pope" was originally bestowed on all bishops, but since the 5th century it has been reserved exclusively for the Bishop of Rome. In the Roman Catholic Church, the Pope has the power of divine institution, because he is the Vicar of Christ and the successor of Saint Peter to whom Christ entrusted the duty of perpetuating his Word "until the end of time."

The authority of the Bishop of Rome was affirmed between the 1st and 4th century. The first known Pontifical Act dates back to the year 96 and was issued by Saint Clement to the Christian community in Corinth. In the 2nd century the Bishop of Carthage, Saint Cyprian, defined the Roman Church as "the central Church from which the unity of the clergy springs." More explicit acknowledgement of Christianity's diffusion throughout the Roman Empire came about with the edict of Milan (313), issued by Emperor Constantine, allowing Christians religious freedom and restoring possessions that had been confiscated from them. Furthermore, the Emperor, for religious vocation and to stabilise the empire, took an active role in ecclesiastical organisation. He nominated bishops in many major cities and is responsible for the construction of several Basilicas, including the ancient Saint Peter's Basilica in the Vatican. He is also credited with calling the Nicene Council (325), the first of 22 Ecumenical councils.

Under the reigns of Constantine and Theodosius (who proclaimed Christianity as the state religion) the temporal power of the Church grew, thanks to gifts from wealthy followers.

Saint Sergius affirmed in 385 that the law of the Roman Church was valid everywhere, while the Council of Calcedonia (451) affirmed that "Peter hath spoken by the mouth of the Pope".

Pope Boniface VIII inaugurantes the first Holy Year in 1300, in a fresco by Giotto.

Drawing of the old St. Peter's Basilica, built by the Emperor Constantine.

Bernini's bronze baldacchino (canopy) above the papal altar.

The statue of St. Peter in front of the Basilica of that name.

At the fall of the Roman Empire in 476, the papacy remained the only power capable of defending the Italian peninsula from the invading barbarians. The pontificate of Saint Leo the Great (440-461) and Saint Gregory the Great (590-604) strengthened the relationship with the new rulers and began the work of spreading Christianity throughout Europe.

Longobard King Liutprando donated Sutri (north of Rome) in 728, to the Church marking the beginnings of the Pontifical State. In the year 755, French King Pepin the Short made ulterior donations following his march into the Italian peninsula to defend Pope Stephen II during the Longobard invasion. French influence reached its apex during the year 800 when Charlemagne was crowned Emperor of the Holy Roman Empire by Pope Saint Leo III.

The decay of the Carolignian Empire (903) and the rise of feudalism weakened the Church immensely. Rome lived through years of siege and battle, which inevitably took its toll on papal power; the period was characterised by weak popes who were at the mercy of stronger factions. The Germanic Emperors, Otto I and Henry III, intervened to strengthen the pontificate of John XIII (965-972) and of Sylvester II (999-1003), but pretended the right to intervene in papal elections and Church life.

Leo IX presided over The council of Reims in 1049, declaring the Rome Bishop as the First Apostle of the universal Church. The Empire's dominance over the Church waned with Nicholas II. He restored the cardinals' right to elect the Pope in 1059. With the famous humiliation of Emperor Henry IV at Canossa (1077) and the edict of Worms (1122) the papacy gained a dominant role in the exercise of spiritual power throughout Europe. Pope Gregory VII (1073-1085) affirmed papal supremacy with his document *Dictatus Papae,* securing the pontifical right to dismiss the emperor. In the 13th century, Pope Innocent III elaborated the theory of "papal theocracy," awarding the Pope spiritual and temporal power. Emperors, whose powers descended directly by divine will, still did not have enough strength to rule without investiture from the Roman Church. The Pope required an act of obedience from nominated bishops and his delegates were present in churches throughout the European continent to ensure that his decrees were carried out. Monasteries held territorial control, while the Pope acted as a Judge in secular disputes, threatening to excommunicate anyone, royal or ecclesiastical, who took a stand different than his own.

The crusades, which began in 1095 under the reign of Urban II, fit perfectly in this context. With Islam occupying the Holy Land, the kingdom united under the symbol of the Holy Cross fighting against a common enemy, which kept feudal contrasts under control.

At the end of the 13th century, the birth of national States (France and England first) and monarchical absolutism, threatened the unity of the Holy Roman Empire and cut deeply into the foundations of pontifical power. French Pope Clement V was pressured by the King of France in 1309 to move the pontifical seat to the city of Avignon in Provence, beginning the "Avignon captivity," which lasted until 1377. During this time the popes were under the tutelage of the King of France. This was followed by the clamorous era of the great Western schism (1378-1417) when two and three popes simultaneously sought the pontifical throne, bringing about heretical and schismatic currents in central Europe.

During the Renaissance (the second half of the 15th century), the Church neglected its spiritual and doctrinal role and fell into merely exercising power. The Pope's hegemonic power ebbed and local discontentment grew, bringing about the rebellion of Luther and Calvin in 1517, which blossomed into the Protestant Reformation. Paul III tried to halt the disintegration of Europe, in 1545, with the council of Trent, which lasted, with various interruptions, until 1563. This resulted in strengthening the papacy and brought about the founding of governing organisations such as the Sant'Uffizio, the Index and new congregations.

During the 17th and 18th century, the curia became very Italian and only Italian popes were nominated until 1978. The affirmation of the large European states brought about a drastic reduction of Papal power, even in Catholic countries. The French Revolution, in 1789, caught the Sainted Seat completely unprepared to affront the far-reaching issues it caused. Napoleon's imperial ambitions partially restored the Church's political role, in 1804, when the Pope crowned him emperor in Notre Dame. The French conquest of Rome in 1809 and the arrest of Pope Pious VII brought about a long period of pontifical detention that would last until 1813.

After the Vienna Congress (1814-1815), the restoration following Napoleon's reign restored temporal power to the Roman Church and the pontifical state (which extended throughout central Italy) and confirmed the role of spiritual leader to the main governing nobility of Europe. However in the 18th century, the difficulty of managing these two roles kept the Pope from truly understanding

A religious ceremony in St. Peter's Basilica.

The 2005 Conclave ended with the election of cardinal Ratzinger (standing on the left) to the papal throne.

Panoramic view of the the Vatican.

the Risorgimento that pervaded the Italian peninsula as well as the central Catholic Hapsburg Empire. The encyclicals published by Gregory XVI and Pius IX against the liberal ideas of the times were written in this context.

The disbanding of the Pontifical State (1870) following the unity of Italy caused the difficult "Roman question" between the Pope and the kingdom of Italy, bringing about the end of the pontificate's temporal power. The voluntary exile of Pius IX, in the Vatican, reshaped the role of the Church in Italy and world politics and limited its power to the sphere of religious doctrine. From that came the first Vatican council's (1870) proclamation of the dogma of papal infallibility and the encyclicals by Leo XIII and Pius X.

Pope Benedict XV (1914-1922) tried, without luck, to convince international communities to desist with the "useless destruction" of the World War I. He did however lay the foundations for the pacifistic policy that has characterised the Church throughout the 20th century.

Pope Pius XI (1922-1939) reached an agreement with the Italian government, led by Mussolini, with the Lateran Pacts (1929), which gave the Church dominion over Vatican City (44 hectares inside the city of Rome) as well as acknowledging Church autonomy in ecclesiastical organisations throughout the Italian territory. World War II and the difficult times following it characterised the pontificate of Pius XII (1939-1958), who wisely opposed the totalitarian, Nazi and Fascist regimes and was a strong enemy of Soviet Russia. He provided the faithful with conservative doctrine to oppose the rapid changes in world society after the war. Pope John XXIII understood that the Church, in order to maintain an important role in society, had to modernise and to change its institutions to fit the necessities of the modern world. After three years of preparation, in 1962 he called the second Vatican council, which would be continued by Paul VI, and which, left a strong mark on Catholic history, determining the organisation of ecclesiastical structures and the fundamental doctrines that characterise today's Church. In 1978, after the short pontificate of John Paul I (August-September), the conclave of cardinals elected Polish Cardinal Karol Wojtyla as Pope. He took the name John Paul II and during his 27-year pontificate, restored the papacy's importance in political and social issues, accelerating the fall of soviet communism and changing the world's political geography. Following the outline of second Vatican council, Pope Wojtyla fixed several points of religious doctrine and reinforced the Catholic world community's bonds with the Sainted Seat, opening dialogue with other religions, and fighting to stop political conflicts from turning into religious wars.

In April 2005, following the trend, another non-Italian Pope was elected. The German Cardinal Ratzinger, took the name Benedict XVI as Pope. Many important questions await him including the necessity to intervene in ecclesiastical organisations, making them more efficient in the modern globalised world.

CHRONOLOGICAL LIST OF THE POPES

1 - St. PETER (67)
2 - (St.) LINUS (67-76)
3 - (St.) ANACLETUS (Ist cen.)
4 - St. CLEMENT I (88-97)
5 - St. EVARISTUS (97-105)
6 - St. ALEXANDER I (105-115)
7 - (St.) SIXTUS I (115-125)
8 - (St.) TELESPHORUS (125-136)
9 - (St.) HYGINUS (136-140)
10 - St. PIUS I (140-155)
11 - (St.) ANICETUS (155-166)
12 - (St.) SOTER (166-175)
13 - St. ELEUTHERIUS (175-189)
14 - St. VICTOR I (189-199)
15 - St. ZEPHYRINUS (199-217)
16 - St. CALLISTUS I (217-22)
17 - St. URBAN I (222-30)
18 - St. PONTIAN (230-35)
19 - St. ANTERUS (235-36)
20 - St. FABIAN (236-50)
21 - St. CORNELIUS (251-53)
22 - (St.) LUCIUS I (253-54)

23 - St. STEPHEN I (254-257)
24 - St. SIXTUS II (257-258)
25 - St. DIONYSIUS (260-268)
26 - St. FELIX I (269-274)
27 - St. EUTYCHIAN (275-283)
28 - (St.) CAIUS (283-296)
29 - St. MARCELLINUS (296-304)
30 - St. MARCELLUS I (308-309)
31 - St. EUSEBIUS (309)
32 - (St.) MILTIADES (311-14)
33 - St. SYLVESTER I (314-35)
34 - St. MARK (336)
35 - St. JULIUS I (337-52)
36 - LIBERIUS (352-66)
37 - St. DAMASUS I (366-84)
38 - St. SIRICIUS (384-99)
39 - St. ANASTASIUS I (399-401)
40 - St. INNOCENT I (401-17)
41 - St. ZOSIMAS (417-18)
42 - St. BONIFACE I (418-22)
43 - St. CELESTINE I (422-32)
44 - (St.) SIXTUS III (432-40)
45 - St. LEO I (the Great) (440-61)
46 - St. HILARIUS (461-68)
47 - St. SIMPLICIUS (468-83)
48 - St. FELIX III (II) (483-92)
49 - St. GELASIUS I (492-96)
50 - (St.) ANASTASIUS II (496-98)
51 - St. SYMMACHUS (498-514)
52 - St. HORMISDAS (514-23)
53 - St. JOHN I (523-26)
54 - St. FELIX IV (III) (526-30)
55 - BONIFACE II (530-32)
56 - JOHN II (533-35)

57 - St. AGAPETUS I (535-36)
58 - St. SILVERIUS (536-37)
59 - VIGILIUS (537-55)
60 - PELAGIUS I (556-61)
61 - JOHN III (561-74)
62 - BENEDICT I (575-79)
63 - PELAGIUS II (579-90)
64 - St. GREGORY I (the Great)(590-604)
65 - SABINIAN (604-606)
66 - BONIFACE III (607)
67 - BONIFACE IV (608-15)
68 - St. ADEODATUS I (615-18)
69 - BONIFACE V (619-25)
70 - HONORIUS I (625-38)
71 - SEVERINUS (640)
72 - JOHN IV (640-42)
73 - THEODORE I (642-49)
74 - St. MARTIN I (649-55)
75 - St. EUGENE I (654-57)
76 - St. VITALIAN (657-72)
77 - ADEODATUS II (672-76)
78 - DONUS (676-78)
79 - St. AGATHO (678-81)
80 - St. LEO II (682-83)
81 - St. BENEDICT II (684-85)
82 - JOHN V (685-86)
83 - CONON (686-87)
84 - St. SERGIUS I (687-701)
85 - JOHN VI (701-05)
86 - JOHN VII (705-07)
87 - SISINNIUS (708)
88 - CONSTANTINE (708-15)
89 - St. GREGORY II (715-31)
90 - St. GREGORY III (731-41)
91 - St. ZACHARY (741-52)
92 - STEPHEN II (III) (752-57)
93 - St. PAUL I (757-67)
94 - STEPHEN III (IV) (767-72)
95 - ADRIAN I (772-95)
96 - St. LEO III (795-816)
97 - STEPHEN IV (V) (816-17)
98 - St. PASCHAL I (817-24)
99 - EUGENE II (824-27)
100 - VALENTINE (827)
101 - GREGORY IV (827-44)

A warm embrace between pope John Paul II and cardinal Ratzinger, future pope Benedict XVI.

102 - SERGIUS II (844-47)
103 - St. LEO IV (847-55)
104 - BENEDICT III (855-58)
105 - St. NICHOLAS I (858-67)
106 - ADRIAN II (867-72)
107 - JOHN VIII (872-82)
108 - MARINUS I (882-84)
109 - St. ADRIAN III (884-85)
110 - STEPHEN V (VI) (885-91)
111 - FORMOSUS (891-96)
112 - BONIFACE VI (896)
113 - STEPHEN VI (VII) (896-97)
114 - ROMANUS
   (August-November, 897)
115 - THEODORE II (897)
116 - JOHN IX (898-900)
117 - BENEDICT IV (900-03)
118 - LEO V (July-September, 903)
119 - SERGIUS III (904-11)
120 - ANASTASIUS III (911-13)
121 - LANDO (913-14)
122 - JOHN X (914-28)
123 - LEO VI (May-September, 928)
124 - STEPHEN VII (VIII) (929-31)
125 - JOHN XI (931-35)
126 - LEO VII (936-39)
127 - STEPHEN VIII (IX) (939-42)
128 - MARINUS II (942-46)
129 - AGAPETUS II (946-55)
130 -JOHN XII (955-63)
131 - LEO VIII (963-64)
132 - BENEDICT V (964-966)
133 - JOHN XIII (965-72)
134 - BENEDICT VI (973-74)
135 - BENEDICT VII (974-83)
136 - JOHN XIV (983-84)
137 - JOHN XV (985-96)
138 - GREGORY V (996-99)
139 - SYLVESTER II (999-1003)
140 - JOHN XVII (1003)
141 - JOHN XVIII (1003-09)
142 - SERGIUS IV (1009-12)
143 - BENEDICT VIII (1012-24)
144 - JOHN XIX (1024-32)
145-147-150- BENEDICT IX (1045)

146 - SYLVESTER III
   (January 20-February 10, 1045)
148 - GREGORY VI (1045-46)
149 - CLEMENT II (1046-47)
151 - DAMASUS II (1048)
152 - St. LEO IX (1049-54)
153 - VICTOR II (1055-57)
154 - STEPHEN IX (X) (1057-58)
155 - NICHOLAS II (1059-61)
156 - ALEXANDER II (1061-73)
157 - St. GREGORY VII (1073-85)
158 - Blessed VICTOR III (1086-87)
159 - Blessed URBAN II (1088-99)
160 - PASCHAL II (1099-1118)
161 - GELASIUS II (1118-19)
162 - CALLISTUS II (1119-24)
163 - HONORIUS II (1124-30)
164 - INNOCENT II (1130-43)
165 - CELESTINE II (1143-44)
166 - LUCIUS II (1144-45)
167 - Blessed EUGENE III (1145-53)
168 - ANASTASIUS IV (1153-54)
169 - ADRIAN IV (1154-59)
170 - ALEXANDER III (1159-81)
171 - LUCIUS III (1181-85)
172 - URBAN III (1185-87)
173 - GREGORY VIII
   (October 25- December 17, 1187)
174 - CLEMENT III (1187-91)
175 - CELESTINE III (1191-98)
176 - INNOCENT III (1198-1216)
177 - HONORIUS III (1216-27)
178 - GREGORY IX (1227-41)
179 - CELESTINE IV
   (October 28-November, 10 1241)
180 - INNOCENT IV (1243-54)
181 - ALEXANDER IV (1254-61)
182 - URBAN IV (1261-64)
183 - CLEMENT IV (1265-68)
184 - Blessed GREGORY X (1271-76)
185 - Blessed INNOCENT V (1276)
186 - ADRIAN V (1276)
187 - JOHN XXI (1276-77)
188 - NICHOLAS III (1277-80)
189 - MARTIN IV (1281-85)
190 - HONORIUS IV (1285-87)
191 - NICHOLAS IV (1288-92)
192 - St. CELESTINE V
   (July 5-December 13,1294)
193 - BONIFACE VIII (1294-1303)
194 - Blessed BENEDICT XI (1303-04)
195 - CLEMENT V (1305-14)
196 - JOHN XXII (1316-34)
197 - BENEDICT XII (1334-42)
198 - CLEMENT VI (1342-52)
199 - INNOCENT VI (1352-62)
200 - Blessed URBAN V (1362-70)
201 - GREGORY XI (1370-78)
202 - URBAN VI (1378-89)
203 - BONIFACE IX (1389-1404)
204 - INNOCENT VII (1404-06)
205 - GREGORY XII (1406-15)
206 - MARTIN V (1417-31)

207 - EUGENE IV (1431-47)
208 - NICHOLAS V (1447-55)
209 - CALLISTUS III (1455-58)
210 - PIUS II (1458-64)
211 - PAUL II (1464-71)
212 - SIXTUS IV (1471-84)
213 - INNOCENT VIII (1484-92)
214 - ALEXANDER VI (1492-1503)
215 - PIUS III
   (September22-October 18,1503)
216 - JULIUS II (1503-13)
217 - LEO X (1513-21)
218 - ADRIAN VI (1522-23)
219 - CLEMENT VII (1523-34)
220 - PAUL III (1534-49)
221 - JULIUS III (1550-55)
222 - MARCELLUS II (1555)
223 - PAUL IV (1555-59)
224 - PIUS IV (1559-65)
225 - St. PIUS V (1566-72)
226 - GREGORY XIII (1572-85)
227 - SIXTUS V (1585-90)
228 - URBAN VII (1590)
229 - GREGORY XIV (1590-91)
230 - INNOCENT IX (1591)
231 - CLEMENT VIII (1592-1605)
232 - LEO XI (1605)
233 - PAUL V (1605-21)
234 - GREGORY XV (1621-23)
235 - URBAN VIII (1623-44)
236 - INNOCENT X (1644-55)
237 - ALEXANDER VII (1655-67)
238 - CLEMENT IX (1667-69)
239 - CLEMENT X (1670-76)
240 - Blessed INNOCENT XI (1676-89)
241 - ALEXANDER VIII (1689-91)
242 - INNOCENT XII (1691-1700)
243 - CLEMENT XI (1700-21)
244 - INNOCENT XIII (1721-24)
245 - BENEDICT XIII (1724-30)
246 - CLEMENT XII (1730-40)
247 - BENEDICT XIV (1740-58)
248 - CLEMENT XIII (1758-69)
249 - CLEMENT XIV (1769-74)
250 - PIUS VI (1775-99)
251 - PIUS VII (1800-23)
252 - LEO XII (1823-29)
253 - PIUS VIII (1829-30)
254 - GREGORY XVI (1831-46)
255 - Blessed PIUS IX (1846-78)
256 - LEO XIII (1878-1903)
257 - St. PIUS X (1903-14)
258 - BENEDICT XV (1914-22)
259 - PIUS XI (1922-39)
260 - PIUS XII (1939-58)
261 - Blessed JOHN XXIII (1958-63)
262 - PAUL VI (1963-78)
263 - JOHN PAUL I
   (August 26-September 28, 1978)
264 - JOHN PAUL II
   (October 16, 1978-April 2, 2005)
265 - BENEDICT XVI
   (April 19, 2005)

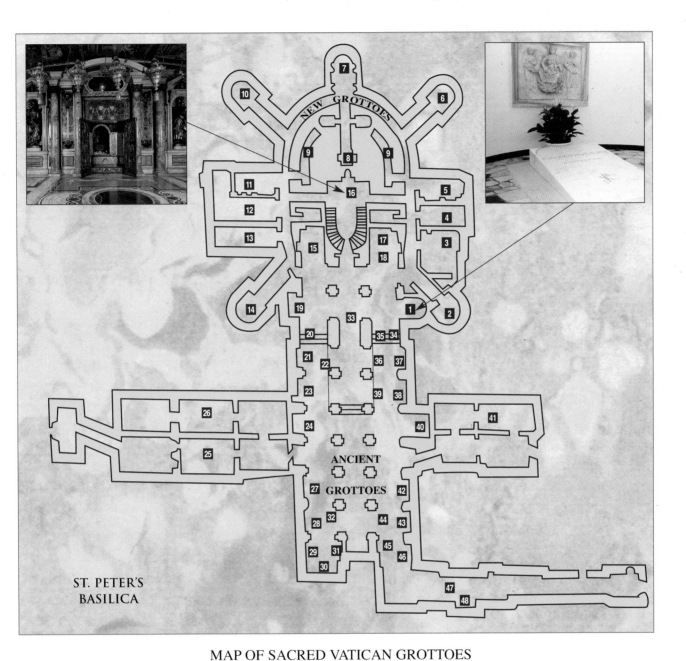

MAP OF SACRED VATICAN GROTTOES

1- Tomb of John Paul II
2- Chapel of Saint Longin
3- Chapel of the Sainted Patrons of Europe
4- Polish Chapel
5- Irish Chapel
6- Chapel of Saint Helena
7- Tomb of Pius XII
8- Chapel of Saint Peter or Clementine
9- Semicircular crypt of Gregory the Great
10- Chapel of Veronica
11- Chapel of the "Maddonna of the Bocciata"
12- Chapel of the East
13- Chapel of Lithuania
14- Chapel of Saint Andrew
15- Mexican Chapel
16- Niche of the pallium over Saint Peter's Tomb

17- Chapel of the Orsini Madonna
18- Tomb of Pius VI
19- Tomb of Pius XI
20- Tomb of Cardinal Merry del Val
21- Tomb of the Stuarts
22- Tomb of Cardinal Frederick Todeschini
23- Tomb Innocent XIII
24- Tomb of Urban VI
25- Antiquarium Hall
26- Antiquarium Hall
27- Cenotaph of Pius III
28- Tomb of Adrian IV
29- Tomb of Gregory V
30- Tomb of Emperor Odo
31- Tomb of Julius III
32- Tomb of Mon. Ludwig Kaas

33- Altar of the Tomb
34- Tomb of Cristina of Sweden
35- Tomb of Queen Carol of Cyprus
36- Tomb of Benedict XV
37- Tomb of Innocent IX
38- Tomb of Marcellus II
39- Tomb of John Paul I
40- Tomb of Paul VI
41- Hungarian Chapel
42- Tomb of Paul II
43- Tomb of Nicholas V
44- Tomb of Innocent VII
45- Tomb of Nicholas III
46- Tomb of Boniface VIII
47- Remains of the dividing wall of Paul III
48- Cenotaph of Callistus III

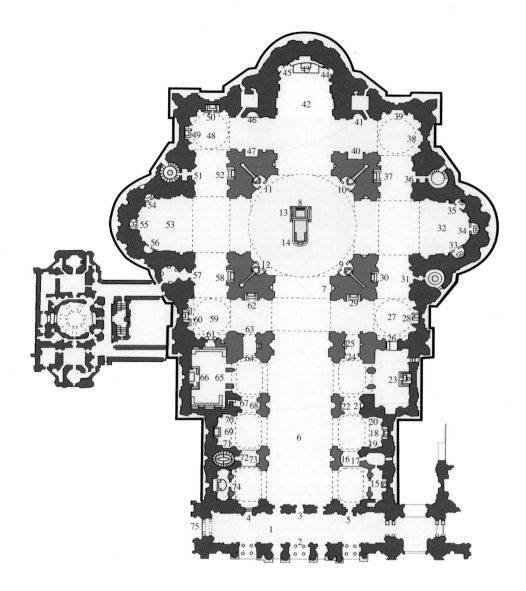

ST. PETER'S BASILICA

1) Atrium. 2) Mosaic of the Navicella. 3) Central Door (Filarete). 4) Door of the Dead (Manzù). 5) Holy Door. 6) Nave. 7) Statue of St. Peter. 8) Papal Altar. 9) Statue of St. Longino. 10) Statue of St. Helena. 11) Statue of Veronica. 12) Statue of St. Andrew. 13) Canopy. 14) Confession. 15) Chapel of the Pietà. 16) Monument to Christine of Sweden. 17) Monument to Leo XII.18) Chapel of St. Sebastian. 19) Monument to Pius XI. 20) Monument to Pius XII. 21) Monument to Innocent XII. 22) Monument to the Countess Mathilde of Canossa. 23) Chapel of the Blessed Sacrament. 24) Monument to Gregory XIII. 25) Monument to Gregory XIV. 26) Monument to Gregory XVI. 27) Gregorian Chapel. 28) Altar of our Lady of Succour. 29) Altar of St. Jerome. 30) Altar of St. Basil. 31) Monument to Benedict XIV. 32) Right transept. 33) Altar of St. Wenceslas. 34) Altar of St. Processus and Martinian. 35) Altar of St. Erasmus. 36) Monument to Clement XIII. 37) Altar of the Incense-boat. 38) Altar of the Archangel Michael. 39) Altar of St. Petronilla. 40) Altar of St. Peter. 41) Monument to Clement X. 42) Nave of the Throne. 43) St. Peter's Throne. 44) Monument to Urban VIII. 45) Monument to Paul III. 46) Monument to Alexander VIII. 47) Altar of St. Peter who's healing the cripple. 48) Chapel of the Column. 49) Altar of the Virgin of the Column. 50) Altar of St. Leo the Great. 51) Monument to Alexander VII. 52) Altar to the Sacred Heart. 53) Left Transept. 54) Altar of St. Thomas. 55) Altar of St. Joseph. 56) Altar of the Crucifixion of St. Peter. 57) Monument to Pius VIII (entrance to Treasure). 58) Altar of the Falsehood. 59) Clementine Chapel. 60) Altar of St. Gregory. 61) Monument to Pius VII. 62) Altar of the Transfiguration. 63) Monument to Leo XI. 64) Monument to Innocent XI. 65) Chapel of the Choir. 66) Altar of the Immaculate Conception. 67) Monument to St. Pius X. 68) Monument to Innocent VIII. 69) Chapel of the Presentation of the Virgin. 70) Monument to John XXIII. 71) Monument to Benedict XV. 72) Monument to Mary Clementine Sobieski. 73) Stuart Monument. 74) Baptistery. 75) Arco delle Campane.